S0-BNA-968

PRINCIPLES OF
FUNCTIONAL PROGRAMMING

PRINCIPLES OF FUNCTIONAL PROGRAMMING

Hugh Glaser
King's College, University of London

Chris Hankin
Imperial College of Science and Technology,
University of London

and
David Till
King's College, University of London

Prentice/Hall PHI **International**

ENGLEWOOD CLIFFS, N.J.   LONDON   NEW DELHI   RIO DE JANEIRO
SINGAPORE   SYDNEY   TOKYO   TORONTO   WELLINGTON

Library of Congress Cataloging in Publication Data

Glaser, Hugh
       Principles of functional programming.
       Bibliography; p.
       Includes index.
       1. Electronic digital computers – Programming.
2. Programming languages (Electronic computers)
I. Hankin, Chris. II. Till, David. III. Title.
QA76.6.H3337   1984   001.64'2   84-8317

ISBN 0-13-709148-6 (cloth)

British Library Cataloging in Publication Data

Glaser, Hugh
       Principles of functional programming.
       1. Electronic digital computers –
       Programming
       I. Title II. Hankin, Chris III. Till, David
       001.64'2 QA76.6

ISBN 0-13-709163-X (pbk.)
ISBN 0-13-709148-6 (cloth)

ISBN 0-13-709163-X {PBK. }
ISBN 0-13-709148-6 {CLOTH}

PRENTICE-HALL INTERNATIONAL INC., London
PRENTICE-HALL OF AUSTRALIA PTY., LTD., Sydney
PRENTICE-HALL CANADA, INC., Toronto
PRENTICE-HALL OF INDIA PRIVATE LIMITED., New Delhi
PRENTICE-HALL OF JAPAN, INC., Tokyo
PRENTICE-HALL OF SOUTHEAST ASIA PTE., Ltd., Singapore
PRENTICE-HALL DO BRASIL LTDA., Rio de Janeiro
WHITEHALL BOOKS LIMITED, Wellington, New Zealand

Printed in Great Britain by SRP Ltd., Exeter

10 9 8 7 6 5 4 3

CONTENTS

v

PREFACE

The last ten years have seen Computer Science reach maturity as an engineering discipline. Extensive efforts have been expended in the development of rigorous methods for specifying, producing and verifying software and hardware products. However, as long as these efforts were restricted to conventional, von Neumann, computers and conventional languages, they fell far short of the ideal. The very nature of the von Neumann approach has contributed to this failure since the notion of a global state that may change arbitrarily at each step of the computation has proved to be both intuitively and mathematically intractable. This failure has made software the most expensive component of many computer systems and this will be compounded by the introduction of large multi-processor systems.

The major costs of software may be apportioned to the five parts of the software life cycle:

1. Specification
2. Design
3. Implementation
4. Testing
5. Operation and Maintenance

While phase 5 is certainly the most costly, much of its cost can be attributed to failure at earlier phases of the cycle. Although formal specification methods do exist, they are not widely used and there is usually a severe mismatch between the levels of language used in the specification, design and implementation phases. Thus the problem of deciding whether a particular program meets a specification usually involves "exhaustive" testing and inevitably leads to software failure, due to undetected errors, during phase 5 of the cycle. The solution to these problems seems to lie in the use of formal specification and design languages, higher level, problem-oriented programming languages and formal correctness proofs.

The first steps in this direction were taken by the structured programming advocates of the early seventies. Work in the areas of formal specification, program verification and formal semantics of programming languages has continued apace since then. A growing number of research workers have realized that many of the problems stem from the fundamental approach of the von Neumann philosophy and are turning to novel languages and computer architectures as a solution. One such approach is that taken by functional programming languages and the related architectures. Some of the claims that have been made for functional programming are:

Functional languages are more problem-oriented than conventional languages: the jump from a formal specification to a functional program is thus much shorter and easier.

Functional languages have a simple mathematical basis, the λ-calculus, and because of the lack of side-effects, program correctness proofs are easier.

Functional programs are generally shorter than their conventional counterparts and thus easier to enhance and maintain.

Functional languages seem to provide one answer to the problem of exploiting the parallelism offered by multiprocessor systems.

Each of these points is a matter for extensive debate; however, it is clear that functional programming will remain an important part of Computer Science in the years to come. A detailed discussion of these claims is beyond the scope of this book but we do hope that the readers will gain sufficient experience of functional programming so that no further convincing is necessary.

The material presented here was used as the basis for a second and third year undergraduate course in the years 1981-82 and 1982-83 and was covered in about thirty one-hour lectures. The course also involved a substantial practical element. The material in the book is largely independent of any particular programming language but it is an advantage to have access to a SUGAR implementation or any other functional language that provides a robust and pleasant interactive environment. We assume the reader has a working knowledge of at least one block-structured language such as PASCAL or ALGOL-68 and an understanding of the principles of structured programming would be an advantage. The aim of the book is to present the concepts at a simple level and so much of the presentation is informal, relying on intuition where possible; references to rigorous treatments of the material are provided at the end of each chapter.

The book is divided into three sections which respectively cover programming, theory and a survey of the functional language landscape. In Part 1 we present a programming methodology for functional programming and a simple functional programming language, SUGAR, which is similar to the notation used by Henderson and others (see the references at the end of Chapter 2). Part 2 presents the theoretical foundations of functional programming and discusses several implementation strategies. Finally, Part 3 surveys the various functional languages that are available, taking a detailed look at LISP and discussing some of the more advanced features of recent languages. There are also a number of appendices that contain useful reference material. A shorter course could be based on Part 1, the first three chapters of Part 2 and, possibly, the first chapter of Part 3.

We thank all of the staff and students at Westfield who have helped us to produce this book, but we note particularly the following for their assistance: David Barnes and Sean Hayes for the implementation of various dialects of SUGAR and their constructive criticisms of early drafts of the text; David Bolton for reading the text and making many useful suggestions, and also his work on the typesetting; Richard Sykes for assistance with the material of Chapter 6; David Turner for allowing us to base the implementation of SUGAR on his implementation of SASL and both David and Peter Henderson for their helpful comments on the text; John Sharp for his work on the design of CAJOLE, the precursor of SUGAR.

Hugh Glaser
Chris Hankin
David Till

Westfield College, July 1984.

PART 1

FUNCTIONAL PROGRAMMING

The aim of this part of the book is to give the reader a thorough grounding in the art of functional programming. We start by discussing a programming methodology and then introduce a very simple programming language and look at a number of different programming examples. Later, in the second and third parts of the text, we shall turn to more theoretical considerations and also discuss some more powerful languages.

The process of programming a solution to a problem is inherently difficult. This has been recognized by conventional programmers for many years and has been one of the motivating forces behind structured programming techniques. The problem seems to be that the human brain does not have the capacity to handle the complexity of the programming task for non-trivial problems. The solution has been to use structured techniques which break the problem up into manageable "chunks". While programs written in functional languages are generally shorter than equivalent conventional programs, for non-trivial tasks the problem of complexity remains and we need a programming methodology to overcome it. In Chapter 1, we introduce a programming methodology that is based on top-down stepwise refinement but has been adapted to the requirements of functional programming.

In Chapter 2, we present a simple functional programming language, SUGAR. This language has been chosen because of its simplicity and similarity to notations used in older books about functional programming. We present several detailed examples of SUGAR programs and there are many exercises.

1

FUNCTIONAL PROGRAM DEVELOPMENT

In this first chapter we are concerned with the process of producing programs in the functional style. Using an analogy, we start by developing functional specifications, comparing them with conventional ones, and then we go on to present methods of designing such specifications. Finally, using these methods, we present an example of the way they can be used in the context of computer programming.

1.1 THE FUNCTIONAL APPROACH

One obvious way to arrange for a system to produce answers to given questions is to supply specific sets of input data and output results for known solutions, and to require the system to infer the more general relationships. Then, using these general relationships, the system solves other specific cases. Although this sort of method has in fact been tried, such systems are not yet sufficiently intelligent to be of general practical use. The most successful and flexible way to make a computer produce the correct results is still to provide a program that explicitly tells the machine what to do.

The form of computer programs varies widely, there being many different languages available. We will consider two particular classes of language that take quite different views of the underlying computer. The more common view is taken by languages such as PASCAL and FORTRAN, and we call these Imperative or Procedural languages. Another view is taken by languages such as SUGAR and "pure" LISP, and these are known as Functional or Applicative languages.

Since the ultimate aims of both types of language are the same, they have much in common, but the differing views of the machine mean that the programming style for each is quite distinct. We believe that the style of programming required for the Functional view of the machine is greatly superior to the traditional style of Imperative languages, and will produce more readable and better documented programs more economically.

We may summarize the differences between the two approaches in the following way:

A program in an Imperative Language is used to convey a list of commands, to be executed in some particular order, such that on completion of the commands the required behavior has been produced.

A program in a Functional Language is used to define an expression which is the solution to a set of problems; this definition can then be used by a machine to produce an answer to a particular problem from the set of problems.

The two approaches, imperative and definitional, can be illustrated by the use of an analogy in which one is asked to specify a physical object. We shall take as an example the specification of a garden shed.

Firstly, one could produce a description of the way in which a shed might be built:

```
To build a shed
          a)   Lay the foundations;
          b)   Build the walls;
          c)   Lay the floor;
          d)   Put the roof on.
```

Secondly, one could produce a description of the structure of a shed in terms of its component parts:

```
A shed consists of
          a)   Walls supported by the foundations;
          b)   A floor supported by the foundations;
          c)   A roof supported by the walls.
```

The imperative (commanding) description of the first approach may be clearly contrasted with the static, definitional description of the second. Both methods provide the required specification of the shed, although the second method has relieved the specifier of telling the builder the order in which he must do things. Thus the explicit ordering of the actions required in the first description has been replaced by an implicit ordering, conditioned by the relationships between the objects, in the second description. The assumption made is that the builder has the intelligence to interpret these relationships correctly. We shall see later that this capacity for interpreting implicit orderings is also a feature of the systems that execute functional languages.

If we now turn our attention to programming languages we see that in an imperative language the sequence of statements means that it is useful to have explicit commands to alter the sequence, for example control structures such as "repeat...until" and "while...do" and of course the "goto". Since the idea of sequencing through a series of statements is not very meaningful in a functional language, not only is it not important in which order a set of statements is written, but also we would not expect to find any statements that attempted to disturb a possible sequence. Thus functional languages do not have such control structures.

This difference between the two sorts of languages gives two particular advantages to the programmer using a functional language. Firstly, the lack of explicit sequence of control relieves the user of the burden of specifying the control flow in the program. Secondly, many errors in imperative languages are introduced because the specified sequencing is not correct, and this question does not arise in functional languages.

EXERCISE

As with the shed analogy, describe a different physical object, for example a bed, using both imperative and definitional approaches.

1.2 TOP-DOWN STEPWISE REFINEMENT

Whatever style of programming is adopted, there is always the same problem in writing significant programs: how are we to specify such large, complex objects? The use of top-down stepwise refinement has been introduced as a very effective tool for developing such large specifications in imperative languages, and we shall find that the method is eminently suitable for functional languages. Indeed one could say that it implies a functional style of programming, and this is recognized in another name for the method, "functional decomposition".

In order to discuss the idea of top-down stepwise refinement we return to the shed analogy of Section 1.1.

Let us first consider the "stepwise refinement" part of "top-down stepwise refinement". Sheds are quite complex objects, and the number of phrases such as "A floor supported by the foundations" that are required to specify every tiny object is enormous. It is, however, actually necessary to make every one of these statements to specify the shed fully. One possibility would be simply to list all the required statements. Clearly this approach, without any structure to it, would probably produce specifications which are both wrong and unreadable.

A more sensible approach would be to arrange for the statements that detail the specification of "walls" to be associated with the statement that introduces "walls". These detailing statements may, of course, require further elaboration and so we produce a hierarchy of statements. A partial specification might thus be represented as a tree as follows:

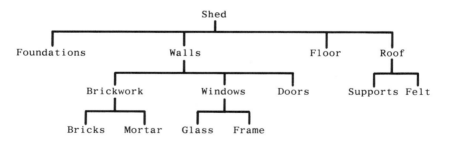

We say that Shed is "refined" as Foundations, Walls, Floor and Roof, and that Roof is "refined" as Supports and Felt and so on. Thus a process of producing such a specification, step by step, would be called "stepwise refinement".

But why "top-down", since the shed itself is presumably not built from the top down?

Since the programmer is creating a structured specification rather than the object itself, the question arises of the order in which such refinements are produced. The phrase "top-down" is intended to imply that this creation process starts, as we have done, from the refinement for Shed, and then proceeds to more detail. Thus everything is referred to before it is defined. This is in contrast to a "bottom-up" approach, in which everything is defined before it is referred to. Note that at any stage during this process the programmer is free to refine any of the objects which require further refinement.

The mechanics of the approach outlined leave us with a clerical problem. A diagram such as that defining Shed cannot easily be created step by step since we need to know the complexity of an object's refinements before we know where to write it on the page. There is a further problem in that at present, as far as computer input is concerned, it is difficult to communicate such a diagram to a machine.

The solution is to specify each refinement in turn as it is produced. If we use ":-" to mean "is refined to" and a number of dashes (-) to terminate refinements, the Shed definition might have been created as follows:

```
Shed  :-
              Foundations;
              Walls;
              Floor;
              Roof
- - - - -
Walls  :-
              Brickwork;
              Windows;
              Doors
- - - - -
Roof    :-
              Supports;
              Felt
- - - - -
Windows  :-
              Glass;
              Frame
- - - - -
Brickwork  :-
              Bricks;
              Mortar
- - - - - -
```

The next step is to produce the detailed, structured definition as required, by "weaving" the individual subrefinements together. This would be best represented by a tree as earlier, but for convenience we shall turn the tree on its side and use indentation to show the different levels.

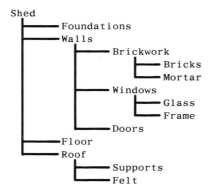

You should satisfy yourself that this process is quite a simple text processing exercise.

It is important to compare the list of refinements with the final specification after weaving and note that both of them are necessary in order to construct a description. The list of refinements satisfies the needs of the dynamic construction process and the final woven specification is the required static description. It can be seen that there is a discrepancy between the order in which we construct a specification and the order in which it is finally presented. The reader will have experienced this problem in conventional languages, and may have used a design language and possibly a program development system. We shall also adopt this solution, which helps to impose a discipline of programming on the user. Our design language will be quite informal, incorporating the idea of top-down stepwise refinement.

EXERCISES

1. Perform some of the refinement process for your physical object from the previous exercise.

2. Weave your refinements together to produce a description.

1.3 FUNCTIONS AND CASES

In practice, of course, sheds vary considerably in both size and design, and we must extend the design language to allow for this. Firstly we note that, depending on the particular application, it may not always be desirable to perform the textual substitution as described above, but rather leave the refinement specification as a definition which can be referenced when necessary. This is particularly true when a refinement is referenced more than once. Clearly if a refinement refers to itself either directly or indirectly (is recursive) then it cannot sensibly be textually substituted. If refinements are referenced in more than one place, it often happens that there are small differences of detail between the requirements of each reference. These differences will be reflected in parameters to the refinements. It should be noted that the addition of parameters to refinements does not preclude performing textual substitution, as before, but in practice we shall leave parameterized refinements as definitions. We shall call such parameterized refinements "functions", since they correspond closely to the mathematical idea of a function. The word function is used in preference to other common terms such as "procedure" and "subroutine" since the refinements are definitional and do not specify the process implied by the other terms. Thus with these new design facilities we might have started to specify the shed more accurately as follows:

```
shed has parameters length, width and height :-
        foundations(width, length) supporting
              floor(width, length) and
              walls supporting
                    roof(width, length)
- - - - -
walls :- wall(side) and wall(back)
         and wall(side) and wall(front)
         joined edge to edge
- - - - -
```

It should be clear from conventional languages that the specification above defines a function "shed" and that there are calls to functions "foundations", "floor", "roof" and "wall". It is interesting to note how in our analogy the concepts that might be termed operators, "supporting" and "joined", connect the defined objects together in a similar way to that in which the operators of programming languages are used.

The final requirement of the design language is the ability to specify alternatives within functions. We use a method known as "case analysis" where each of the possible alternatives are identified and the appropriate definition is associated with each case. An example of this might be the following definition of "wall":

```
wall has parameter sort :-
        when sort is side
        then brickwork(length, height) with a window,
        when sort is front
        then brickwork(width, height) with a door,
        when sort is back
        then brickwork(width, height)
- - - - -
```

Note that in the final production of the design we will require that the function "wall" has access to the parameters of "shed".

If we now leave the analogy and consider some examples of more familiar programming use we find that it is possible to use the same sort of constructs. First we show two examples of function specification:

```
sumsq is the function taking two parameters,
      say par1 and par2, and delivering the sum of the squares
- - - - -
the function taking two parameters, say par1 and par2,
                    and delivering the sum of the squares :-
              [par1, par2]  par1 * par1  +  par2 * par2
- - - - -
pay is the function with parameters the hourly rate
                              hours worked as normal time
                              hours worked as overtime
              and delivering the week's pay :-
pay is [rate, normal, overtime]
              ( normal * rate ) + ( overtime * enhanced rate )
- - - - - - -
enhanced rate :-
                    rate * 3 / 2
- - - - - - -
```

We have introduced here the SUGAR notation for function specification; the single expression that is the body of the function is preceded by the list of formal (or dummy) parameters, enclosed in square brackets.

In making the textual substitution to weave this development together it is useful if the refinement names become comments (between the "#" symbols below), so that the final specification is:

```
sumsq is # the function taking two parameters and delivering
                    the sum of the squares #
           [par1, par2]  par1 * par1  +  par2 * par2;
# pay is the function with parameters the hourly rate
                              hours worked as normal time
                              hours worked as overtime
             and delivering the week's pay #
pay is [rate, normal, overtime]
             ( normal * rate ) + ( overtime * # enhanced rate #
                                              rate * 3 / 2 )
```

The "is" symbol, associating names with their corresponding values, and the ";" to separate definitions are used here since they are the symbols that are used in SUGAR.

One problem with the approach outlined above is that it entails a lot of typing, particularly as refinement names are written out at least twice, firstly at the initial reference and secondly at the definition. To abbreviate previously used names it is useful to employ ellipses (...) to stand for missing text, as we shall see later. The comment produced during the weaving should always be the full text, however.

A small example of the use of case analysis for a programming problem might be as follows:

```
sign is the one parameter function delivering 1, 0 or −1
            according to whether the parameter is
            positive, zero or negative
- - - - -
the one parameter ... negative :-
          [par]  when par > 0 then 1,
                 when par = 0 then 0,
                 when par < 0 then −1
- - - - -
```

Clearly it is important that all expected conditions are dealt with, so that the function is not left undefined in some case. We can see that the function above satisfies this requirement. One further requirement of our method of design is that the conditions should all be mutually exclusive. That is, for a given evaluation of this "case expression", no two conditions evaluate to true. This constraint is important since, although the cases are ordered on the page, they may not be executed in that order in a particular target language. Thus it would be impossible to predict which of the corresponding expressions would be chosen as the value. In general the programmer should choose the most convenient ordering for the cases.

It is sometimes particularly hard to ensure that all cases have been considered, especially when what is required is a case to catch exceptional circumstances and programming errors, which by definition the programmer has forgotten about. A special case, "otherwise", is provided to solve this problem, and this case must appear last if it appears at all.

As an example, the function "sign" might have been written (less clearly) as follows using "otherwise".

```
sign is
            [par]     when par > 0 then 1,
                      when par = 0 then 0,
                      otherwise       −1
- - - - -
```

The developments above have all used a deliberately informal approach in their formulation. This is because developments are merely "scratch pads" for programmers to order their thoughts and need only be clear to humans, not necessarily to computers. The style of the development process may well vary slightly according to the application being programmed, and will often vary in order to take account of the particular facilities available in different languages. It is worth remembering that program development is performed by individuals in their own personal way, and hence does not always benefit from strict, formal notations.

Bearing all this informality in mind, there is a major advantage to be gained from using a formal design language, and that is that the computer can be used to help to automate the process. As we have already noted, the weaving process shown above could, with a little more rigorous definition, be achieved by simple text substitution.

EXERCISES

1. For the object which you defined in the Exercise of Section 1.1, consider how you would improve your specification using functions and cases.

2. Refine the following phrases:

> a) magnitude is the function that delivers the absolute value of its single parameter

> b) max is the function that delivers the value of the largest of its three parameters

1.4 AN EXAMPLE

To illustrate our method we now design a larger program. In order to try to give the reader some feel for the dynamic process involved, we shall step through the way such a design might progress, including the mistakes that may happen and improvements that may be added.

The problem we wish to solve is how to print out an integer as its equivalent in English words. For example, when given the parameter "369", the program should return "three hundred and sixty-nine".

The first thing to do is write down the top-level statement of the problem.

```
engint is the function taking one integer parameter
           and returning the English phrase for that number
--------
```

This may seem rather unnecessary, but it is important to have a clearer statement of the requirements than the English used to explain the problem. In fact, if the refinement process is done properly, each statement should seem like a trivial step; only by making sure each step is very small can mistakes be avoided. It should be clear that if each refinement is correct in isolation then the overall correctness of the design will be assured.

Continuing the refinement process, almost immediately we see some of the problems that will arise in the later stages of refinement; for example, we might become concerned about how to print out the word corresponding to a single digit. There is a great temptation to digress from the strict top-down approach and become involved in how this might be done, even going so far as to produce a function to do it. This temptation should be resisted for two reasons. Firstly, we may eventually find that the initial analysis is wrong and there is no need for such a function. Secondly, the function produced may not fit the eventual requirement perfectly; if this happens the temptation is to distort the design in an attempt to accommodate the function so that the final description no longer represents the natural solution to the problem. This almost inevitably leads to further alterations until the program becomes quite unsatisfactory.

As soon as we begin to think about the first steps of the solution, the question of the range of numbers to be dealt with arises. To answer the question we should be able to look back to the statement of the problem, but clearly we did not make this specific enough. So we need to restate the problem, having considered the range which the program will accept and we also continue to the first level of refinement.

```
engint is the function taking one parameter which should be
             in the range 999 to -999 and returning the
             English phrase for that number
- - - - - -
the function ... English phrase for that number :-
      [number] when number <  -999 then "number too small",
             when number >   999 then "number too large",
             otherwise                valid number string
- - - - -
```

We have enclosed literal strings in double quotes (") to distinguish
them from refinement identifiers and other words.

We now refine "valid number string".

```
valid number string is
      when number < 0 then minus followed by the phrase for
                           the absolute value,
      when number = 0 then "zero",
      when number > 0 then the phrase for the positive number
- - - - -
minus followed ... value is
      "minus " && positive number(-number)
- - - - -
the phrase for the positive number is
      positive number(number)
- - - - - - - -
```

An unfamiliar operator, "&&", has been used here. We shall see later
that this is quite a general operator in SUGAR but here in the design
we are using it to concatenate two strings. The result of the expression
above will be the string "minus ", including the space, followed by the
string that will be returned from the call of "positive number".

There are now no more unrefined phrases left, so in a sense we
have finished the program. Of course this would only be true if the
function "positive number" was already defined. Clearly this is not the
case, and what has happened is that we have produced a slightly
simpler subproblem.

So now we proceed with a possible solution of the subproblem,
which itself generates further subproblems.

```
positive number is the function that given a positive number
                less than a thousand delivers the corresponding
                English phrase
- - - - - - -
the function that given a positive number less than a thousand
        delivers the corresponding English phrase :-
        [posi] hundreds(posi) && tens(posi) && units(posi)
- - - - - - - -
hundreds is the function that returns the string representing
        any hundreds that may be significant in the parameter
- - - - - - - -
the function ... hundreds ... parameter :-
 [numb] when numb > 99 then digit (numb % #integer division#
                                               100)
                              && " hundred",
        when numb <=99 then ""
- - - - - - -
```

Unfortunately before we proceed with the definition of "tens" we realize that it is difficult to decide when there is a requirement for an "and" to be inserted. The natural place to put this is in the definition of "positive number", so we must amend that original definition. This leads us to think more carefully about a possible separator between the tens and units, and we realize it is more sensible to work out the numbers of hundreds, tens and units before passing them to the appropriate selecting functions. We note that the numbers less than twenty are special and we shall deal with them at the same time as "units". Thus the revised function is as follows:

```
positive number is the function that given a positive number
                less than a thousand delivers the corresponding
                English phrase :-
positive number is [posi]
        hundreds string(hundreds) &&
        possible and &&
        tens string(tens) &&
        possible dash &&
        units string(units or teens)
- - - - - - -
hundreds string is [numb]
        when numb > 0 then units string(numb) && " hundred",
        when numb = 0 then ""
- - - - - - -
possible and :-
        when hundreds > 0
         and ( tens > 0  or  units > 0 ) then " and ",
        otherwise  ""
- - - - - -
```

```
tens string is [number]
        when number < 2 then "",
        when number > 1 then the strings twenty,...,ninety
                             indexed by number minus one
........
```

Note that the string for "ten" is empty since we will deal with that separately as a unit.

We now continue refinement, starting with the function "units string" and continuing with "possible dash". Finally we need to define "hundreds", "tens", "units or teens" and "units".

```
units string is [number]
        when number = 0 then "",
        when number > 0 then the strings one,...,nineteen
                             indexed by number
........
possible dash is
        when tens > 1 and units > 0 then "-",
        otherwise         ""
........
hundreds is posi % 100
.......
tens is ( posi % 10 ) - ( hundreds * 10 )
.......
units or teens is when tens = 1 then units + 10,
                  otherwise        units
.......
units is posi - ( tens * 10 ) - ( hundreds * 100 )
.......
```

We have now completed all the refinements except for the actual choosing of the strings, and we leave this unspecified as it will entirely depend on the facilities available in the target language. We now summarize the complete development.

```
engint is the function taking one parameter which should be
             in the range 999 to -999 and returning the
             English phrase for that number
......
the function ... English phrase for that number :-
        [number] when number < -999 then "number too small",
             when number >  999 then "number too large",
             otherwise               valid number string
.....
valid number string is
        when number < 0 then minus followed by the phrase for
                             the absolute value,
        when number = 0 then "zero",
```

```
        when number > 0 then the phrase for the positive number
- - - - -
minus followed ... value is
        "minus " && positive number(-number)
- - - - -
the phrase for the positive number is
        positive number(number)
- - - - - - - -
positive number is the function that given a positive number
                less than a thousand delivers the corresponding
                English phrase :-
positive number is [posi]
        hundreds string(hundreds) &&
        possible and &&
        tens string(tens) &&
        possible dash &&
        units string(units or teens)
- - - - - - -
hundreds string is [numb]
        when numb > 0 then units string(numb) && " hundred",
        when numb = 0 then ""
- - - - - - -
possible and :-
        when hundreds > 0
         and ( tens > 0  or  units > 0 ) then " and ",
        otherwise   ""
- - - - - -
tens string is [number]
        when number < 2 then "",
        when number > 1 then the strings twenty,...,ninety
                                indexed by number minus one
- - - - - - - -
units string is [number]
        when number = 0 then "",
        when number > 0 then the strings one,...,nineteen
                                indexed by number
- - - - - - - -
possible dash is
        when tens > 1 and units > 0 then "-",
        otherwise        ""
- - - - - - - -
hundreds is posi % 100
- - - - - - -
tens is ( posi % 10 ) - ( hundreds * 10 )
- - - - - - -
units or teens is when tens = 1 then units + 10,
                  otherwise       units
- - - - - - -
units is posi - ( tens * 10 ) - ( hundreds * 100 )
- - - - - - -
```

EXERCISES

1. Design a function that returns the string which is the Roman numeral equivalent of its parameter,

$$e.g. \ roman(369) \ gives \ \text{“CCCLXIX”}$$

2. Design a function that delivers the day of the week on which a particular date falls. You will need to use a reference date and day,

$$e.g. \ day(1,1,1983) \ gives \ \text{“Saturday”}$$

3. With reference to Exercises 1 and 2, consider the following questions:

> a) Was the design process quick and easy?
> b) Did it seem to obscure possible errors, or help you to notice them?
> c) On completion of the design, did you have faith in its correctness?
> d) Would it be easy to alter and maintain the program?

BIBLIOGRAPHY

Many texts on programming include discussion of the ideas of structured programming and top-down stepwise refinement, although they approach the subject from the point of view of conventional languages. The seminal work on structured programming is Dahl et al., and on stepwise refinement Wirth. Henderson introduced the method of case analysis into functional programming and provides a readable, detailed treatment.

[Dah] Dahl O.-J., Dijkstra E.W. and Hoare C.A.R. "Structured Programming", Academic Press, 1972.

[Hen] Henderson P. "Functional Programming: Application and Implementation", Prentice-Hall International, 1980.

[Wir] Wirth N. "Program Development by Stepwise Refinement", Communications of the ACM, Vol. 14, pp. 221-227, April 1971.

2

SUGAR:
A SIMPLE FUNCTIONAL LANGUAGE

In the last chapter we produced the design for a significant program, but stopped short of translating that design into a target language. In this chapter, as an introduction to SUGAR, we will show how this translation may be performed. We will then specify the language more accurately, defining the syntax (written form of program) first and then going on to discuss the semantics (what happens when the program is executed). Unfortunately the rigorous definition of the semantics of programming languages is always more complicated than the definition of the syntax, and although functional languages do permit quite concise definition of semantics, we must leave this until the later chapters. For the moment we will approach the semantics of SUGAR by discussing each of the important issues in turn. Finally, we present further examples of SUGAR programs.

2.1 A SUGAR PROGRAM

During the development of "engint", from Chapter 1, we bore in mind that the target language would in fact be SUGAR, and so we would expect that it should be a simple task to translate that design into SUGAR. This is indeed the case, but there are three areas where changes need to be made.

Firstly, since the design language is informal and intended primarily for human consumption, there may be aspects of the design that are not sufficiently rigorous for a computer language. Secondly,

19

there will be refinements in the design that depend so closely on the facilities available in the particular target language that they have been left incomplete. Thirdly, the refinements need to be woven together to form the program.

The simplest of the changes required is because spaces are not permitted in identifiers in SUGAR. Instead the underline character ( ) is usually used to join words together. Thus "valid number string" must become "valid_number_string". Another syntactic change is required because the case analysis construct in SUGAR does not use the keyword "when", but rather uses various keywords starting with the keyword **if**. The reason for this is that the evaluation of cases in SUGAR proceeds in a sequential manner, and thus the use of "when" might be misleading. So, for example, the refinement of "hundreds string" produces the following definition in SUGAR:

```
hundreds_string is [numb]
        if   numb > 0 then units_string(numb) && " hundred"
        elsf numb = 0 then ""
        endf
- - - - -
```

The **elsf** is short for "or else if" and is usually read "elsif". The **endf** is used to close the whole expression.

In the design of "engint" we left two of the refinements undefined because they depended strongly on the facilities available in the target language. We can now complete their refinement, for example:

```
the strings twenty,...,ninety indexed by number minus one :-
        <"twenty", "thirty", "forty", "fifty", "sixty",
         "seventy", "eighty", "ninety"> (number − 1)
- - - - -
```

This is an example of the use of a list. We are permitted to index lists (in this case by the value of "number − 1") and so here the list is being used in a similar way to an array in a conventional language.

Finally we must weave the design into a complete program. In doing this we have a further consideration to those mentioned in Section 1.3, and that is the possibility of attaching subdefinitions to expressions, using the **where** construct. This construct introduces scoping rules quite similar to those of blocks in conventional languages, by adding definitions, introduced by the keyword **where**, to an expression and enclosing the whole in braces ("{" and "}"). Note that we do not always attach subdefinitions using a **where**, but sometimes choose to add the auxiliary definitions at the same level as the expression. Often the choice is only governed by the question of readability of the program, and the programmer must decide whether introducing further levels increases or decreases clarity.

In the case of refinements and functions that are referenced more than once the question of where to put the definitions so that all the necessary expressions can access them is more complicated. It is of course simplest if there is a computerized system for weaving the refinements together, and this works out the correct place. Failing this, the programmer must decide on the most logical place that actually allows the correct references. We shall look at the rules for scoping in more detail in Section 2.4.

```
engint is # the function taking one parameter which should
            be in the range 999 to −999 and returning the
            English phrase for that number #
  [number]
  {  if    number < −999 then "number too small"
     elsf number >  999 then "number too large"
     else                    valid_number_string
     endf
  where
    valid_number_string is
      if    number < 0
      then # minus followed by the phrase for
            the absolute value #
            "minus " && positive_number(−number)
      elsf number = 0 then "zero"
      elsf number > 0 then # the phrase for the
                             positive number #
                             positive_number(number)
      endf;
    # positive_number is the function that given a
      positive number less than a thousand delivers the
      corresponding English phrase #
    positive_number is [posi]
          { hundreds_string(hundreds) && possible_and
            && tens_string(tens) && possible_dash
            && units_string(units_or_teens)
          where
            hundreds_string is [numb]
                  if    numb > 0
                  then units_string(numb) && " hundred"
                  elsf numb = 0 then ""
                  endf;
            possible_and is
                  if    hundreds > 0 and
                        ( tens>0 or units>0 ) then " and "
                  else ""
                  endf;
```

```
tens_string is [number]
    if   number < 2
    then ""
    elsf number > 1
    then # the strings twenty,...,ninety indexed
             by number minus one #
           <"twenty","thirty","forty",
            "fifty","sixty","seventy",
            "eighty","ninety">  ( number-1 )
    endf;
units_string is [number]
    if   number = 0
    then ""
    elsf number > 0
    then # the strings one,...,nineteen indexed
             by number #
           <"one","two","three","four","five",
            "six","seven","eight","nine","ten",
            "eleven","twelve","thirteen","fourteen",
            "fifteen","sixteen","seventeen",
            "eighteen","nineteen"> ( number )
    endf;
possible_dash is
    if tens>1 and units>0 then "-" else "" endf;
hundreds is posi % 100;
tens is ( posi % 10 ) - ( hundreds * 10 );
units_or_teens is
    if tens=1 then units + 10 else units endf;
units is posi - (tens * 10) - (hundreds * 100)
}
};
```

2.2 SIMPLE SYNTAX

A program in SUGAR is a list of definitions. As we have seen, each definition associates a SUGAR name with an expression. We use a modified Backus Naur Form in which the non-terminals (those symbols that do not appear in the input) are distinguished by an initial upper case letter. When a non-terminal has "_list" appended this indicates that it may possibly be repeated using a separator of some kind. We define Program as follows:

```
Program    ::=  Definition_list ;
Definition ::=  Name  is  Expression
```

The separator between Definitions is semi-colon (;).

Next we examine Expression. It is important to understand the complete generality of SUGAR Expressions. Any type of Expression can be used anywhere an Expression is required. Once the reader has understood the various ways in which Expressions can be constructed, most of the syntax of the language will be understood. In many languages there are restrictions on the forms of expression that can be used in a particular context; there are no such restrictions in SUGAR. There follow some examples of Expressions:

```
5                                                  (E1)
"abc"                                              (E2)
jim                                                (E3)
c + 5                                              (E4)
f(a)                                               (E5)
[n] n+1                                            (E6)
{ days + day where day is 1; days is 7 }           (E7)
[n] { n+m where m is n+1 }                         (E8)
```

Expressions E1 and E2 are the usual types of literals (integer and string respectively) found in most computer languages, and E3 is an identifier. E4 is a normal arithmetic Expression and E5 represents the application (call) of the function "f" with actual parameter "a". E6 is a more interesting form of Expression and represents a function which at the moment has no name (it may or may not be given one). It is quite permissible to construct such a function simply by listing the formal parameters, followed by the Expression which is the function body, and it can be used anywhere (meaningful) that an Expression is required. For example, if we note that the "f" in E5 was simply an Expression itself, it will be seen that the following is a rather awkward way of specifying the value 2:

```
( [n] n+1 ) (1)
```

The brackets are necessary to make sure that the function body is associated correctly with the formal parameter (see next section).

Expression E7 shows the **where** construct. Here we associate two subdefinitions with the Expression "days+day", thus forming a new Expression. Finally E8 shows how complex Expressions are constructed.

There are two further types of Expression in SUGAR, the conditional expression and the list, of which we saw examples in "engint". To summarize the various possibilities for Expression we list their syntax below:

```
Expression    ::=  Literal
                 | Name
                 | ( Expression )
                 | if Expression then Expression Alternatives
                 | < Element_list > | <>
                 | " Char_list "  |   ""
                 | Expression ( Expression_list )
                 | Op Expression
                 | Expression Op Expression
                 | { Expression where Definition_list }
                 | [ Formal_list ] Expression
```

The normal separator between repeated items is comma (,), but semi-colon (;) is used to separate Definitions. The Literals defined are the real numbers (which include the integers), represented in the conventional manner, the truth values, represented by the words "true" and "false", and single characters, which are identified by a preceding single quote (e.g. 'a and '5 represent the characters "a" and "5" respectively).

We define Alternatives in such a way that we are allowed any number of **elsf**s and an optional **else**. Each formal parameter is a single Name, but predictably Elements are made up of general expressions.

```
Alternatives ::=  else Expression endf
                | elsf Expression then Expression Alternatives
                | endf
Formal       ::=  Name
Element      ::=  Expression
```

As a final remark on the syntax of SUGAR, we note that comments (enclosed in "#"s) can appear anywhere except within Names or Literals, and that identifiers must start with a letter and continue with a possibly empty string of letters or digits or the underline character.

A complete definition of the syntax of SUGAR, together with a list of operators, may be found in Appendix 1.

EXERCISE

Identify at least one of each of the alternatives for Expression from "engint".

2.3 BRACKETING EXPRESSIONS

The above syntax is clearly ambiguous; for example, consider the different ways the following Expression might be understood:

```
[n] n + f (m)
```

The formal parameter alone could be associated with three possible different Expressions ("n", "n+f" or "n+f(m)"). The rules for deciding on the correct associations have been created to give the effect which seems most logical, but of course if there is any doubt then brackets should be introduced.

Ambiguity may arise when a construct does not have distinguishing symbols at both the start and end, and this occurs with four of the possible ways of constructing Expressions. There is a priority system, similar to that for arithmetic Expressions in conventional languages, and the order is that in which the different constructs appear in the definition of Expression. Thus, if we were to bracket an Expression to make the meaning explicit, it should be done with the following binding priorities:

```
1. Function applications.
2. Monadic operators (one operand).
3. Dyadic operators (two operand), but also allowing
              for operator priority.
4. Function specification.
```

Applying the bracketing process to the earlier example we get the following steps:

```
  [n]   n+ f(m)
  [n]   n+(f(m))
  [n] ( n+(f(m)) )
( [n] ( n+(f(m)) ) )
```

This verifies what would usually be the intended meaning of such an Expression.

EXERCISE

Fully bracket the following two Expressions using the above method:

```
a)   [age] { not leap (year−age) where year is now }
```

```
b)    if a < b  then x
      elsf a >= b then y + { z (3)
                          where z is [n] n + 1 }
      endf
```

2.4 RESULT OF AN EXPRESSION

As we have seen a program consists of a list of Definitions. Such a list on its own, however, is a static object that does very little until some request is made to use the Definitions. In order to get anything out of a SUGAR system we present it with an Expression to be evaluated, and this will often be a function application. The system can then use the Definitions it has to evaluate the Expression. Thus to use "engint" we must present an Expression such as the following to the system:

```
engint ( 493 ) ?
```

We terminate the Expression with a question mark (?), rather than a semi-colon, to remind us that it is an Expression to be evaluated and not a Definition. In SUGAR there are no explicit input or output instructions. The input to a program is the parameters, and the output is the result delivered after execution. Either the parameters or the result may themselves be complicated functions, and so this mechanism is quite sophisticated. Another example shows a complete (trivial) program and request for execution.

```
add is [v] v(1) + v(2);
inp is [n] if n=1 then 3 else 4 endf;
add(inp) + 1 ?
```

Note that since any legal SUGAR Expression is permitted, we are not restricted to simple function applications. (The result printed here would be "8".)

In practice, in a pleasant interactive environment such as that in which SUGAR is designed to be used, a session at the terminal will consist of such Definitions and Expressions intermixed, corresponding to the user's requirements at each stage.

To introduce the ideas of evaluation of Expressions we show a walkthrough of the above small program. Indentation is used to indicate subcomputations and the arrow, <----, is used to indicate the return of a value, possibly through more than one level.

```
associate  [v] v(1) + v(2)  with  add
associate  [n]if n=1 then 3 else 4 endf  with  inp
evaluate  add(inp) + 1
    evaluate  add(inp)
        associate  inp  with  v
        call add
            evaluate  v(1) + v(2)
                evaluate  v(1)
                evaluate  inp(1)
                    associate  1  with  n
                    call inp
                        evaluate if n=1 then 3 else 4 endf
                        evaluate if 1=1 then 3 else 4 endf
                        remove association of  n
                <------- 3
                evaluate  v(2)
                evaluate  inp(2)
                    associate  2  with  n
                    call inp
                        evaluate if n=1 then 3 else 4 endf
                        evaluate if 2=1 then 3 else 4 endf
                        remove association of  n
                <------- 4
        remove association of  v
    <----------- 7
<-- 8
print  8
```

We now look in more detail at each type of Expression in turn and examine the way the results are computed.

2.4.1 Literal

The result of evaluation of a Literal is simply the object denoted.

2.4.2 Name

The result of a Name is the result of the Expression with which it has been associated. This association may have been established either in a Definition or by the correspondence between formal and actual parameters during a function call.

2.4.3 Bracketed Expression

The result of a Bracketed expression is simply the result of the enclosed Expression.

2.4.4 Conditional Expression

The result of a Conditional expression is found as follows. Firstly, the Expressions that are the conditions are evaluated in order until one of them evaluates to "true". Secondly, the Expression that follows the appropriate **then** is evaluated, and the result of that Expression is the result of the Conditional expression. If none of the conditions is "true" then, if there is an **else** part, this Expression is evaluated and the result of that Expression is the result of the Conditional Expression. If none of the conditions evaluates to "true" and there is no **else** part then it is an error. For example, consider the following two Definitions using Conditional expressions:

```
ge1 is if   n > 0 then a
        else b
        endf;
ge2 is if   n > 0 then a
        elsf n = 0 then b
        endf;
```

To find the result of "ge1", first find whether "n" is positive; if so, the result is the result of "a". If "n" is not positive the result is the result of "b".

To find the result of "ge2", first find whether "n" is positive; if so, the result is the result of "a". Then find whether "n" is zero and if so the result is the result of "b". If neither of these conditions is true then the result is undefined and there is an error.

2.4.5 Lists

Most computer languages provide methods of collecting together a number of objects into an aggregate such that it can then be referred to as a whole. SUGAR is designed to be a small language and provides only one significant method of helping the programmer to aggregate objects, the List. A larger language might provide more sophisticated data structuring facilities or allow programmer-defined data structuring, as in the language HOPE (see Chapter 8).

We have already seen how Lists may be specified by listing the elements and also how they may be indexed by an integer to find the result of a particular Element. In addition there are four operators associated with the use of Lists: prefix (":") and concat ("&&") for construction, and head ("hd") and tail ("tl") for access. Details of these may be found later in this section. The result of a List expression is the list of results of its elements. Note that the Expression "<>" is used to represent the List with no elements.

2.4.6 Strings

Since the programmer often needs to specify Lists of characters, a variation of the List notation is provided so that such strings can be easily defined. Strings are enclosed in the double quote character ("). A string is still only a shorthand notation for a List of characters, and thus the following definitions of "s1" and "s2" define the same string:

```
s1 is "test";
s2 is <'t, 'e, 's, 't>;
```

For the non-printing characters, such as newline, an alternative representation within strings is provided; the backslash character is used as an escape so that, for example, newline is "\n".

2.4.7 Function Application

The result of a function application is found as follows. Firstly, there may be sufficient actual parameters provided to match all the formal parameters. In this case the Names of the formal parameters are associated with the actual parameters, in order, and the result of the function is the result of evaluating the Expression which is the function body using these associations. Secondly, when there are not sufficient actual parameters for all the formal parameters, the result is a new function which informally can be thought of as "remembering" associations between the formal parameters and the actual parameters provided and as "waiting" for the final set of actual parameters before it evaluates its body.

The experienced programmer will notice that no mention has been made of the parameter evaluation mechanism. Is it "call-by-value" or "call-by-reference" or perhaps even "call-by-name"? Careful thought will show that since, in SUGAR, there are no directly addressable memory cells with changing values, the result of a function is independent of the calling mechanism, although whether it produces a result at all does vary. Since this question of which parameter mechanism to use is quite complex, and is also closely tied to implementation considerations, we shall leave discussion of this topic until later chapters. The label applied to the mechanism in SUGAR is in fact "lazy evaluation".

2.4.8 Monadic Operators

The normal monadic operators evaluate in the usual way when given an operand of the correct type. The operators defined in SUGAR are "+" and "−", requiring numbers as their operands, and "not" which requires a truth value. There are two operators, "hd" (head) and "tl" (tail), that access Lists. The operator "hd" delivers the first element of a List and "tl" delivers the List that remains after the first element has been removed (this may be empty). Finally there is an operator, "atom", that examines its operand to see if it is a structured object; thus it returns "false" if its operand is a list, and "true" otherwise.

2.4.9 Dyadic Operators

Dyadic operators evaluate in the usual way, and are listed in Appendix 1. There are two operators, ":" (prefix) and "&&" (concat), that are used to construct Lists. We introduced the concatenation operator in Chapter 1 where it was used in a restricted way to concatenate strings of characters. In its general form it takes two Lists as operands and the result is another List which is formed from the concatenation of the two operands. Thus the following three Lists are equivalent:

```
( i )        <a, b, c, d>
( ii )       <a, b> && <c, d>
( iii )      <a> && <b, c> && <d>
```

Note that in (iii) the angle brackets are required around "a" and "d" to make them into Lists.

The prefix operator is similar to "concat", but does not expect its left operand to be a List. Thus (iii) could also have been written:

```
a : <b, c> && <d>
```

2.4.10 Auxiliary Definitions

The result of an Expression with auxiliary Definitions is the result of evaluating that Expression using all the current associations of Names with Expressions, augmented by the associations implied by the auxiliary Definitions.

2.4.11 Function

The result of a function expression is simply the function specification formed from the Formals and the Expression. Thus it can be thought of as the object which performs the specified function; we discuss the value of a function at length elsewhere.

2.5 NAMES AND VALUES

We have already said that a SUGAR program is a list of Definitions of the values to be associated with the given Names, and this is also true of the lists of Definitions associated with those Expressions that have **where** clauses. In order that no ambiguity should arise about the Expression associated with a given Name, there may be only one applicable Definition for any particular Name. Thus it should be clear why the following Definition would be illegal:

```
# ILLEGAL DEFINITION #
        jim is { a + b
                where a is c + 2;
                      c is 2;
                      b is c * 3;
                      c is 4
                };
```

In the above, there is no rule to tell us which of the Definitions of "c" are being referred to by the Expressions for "a" and "b". In fact there are four possible Expressions that might be associated with "jim", and this is clearly an undesirable situation.

There are occasions, however, when there may be a number of different associations of a Name available and there are rules, similar to the scoping rules of conventional languages, which allow resolution of the possible confusion. A simple example of this might be the references to "a" in the following program:

```
        m is [a] { a + y
                where y is { k + a where a is 2 };
                      k is 3
                };
```

The first reference to "a" allows no confusion since the only association of "a" that could be sensibly made available in that Expression is that of the Formal. The second reference to "a", on the other hand, could either be the Formal or the "a" defined in the

where clause attached to that Expression. In fact in these circumstances the reference that is assumed is the one from the **where** clause. Thus the program defines the function that returns the value of its actual parameter plus 5.

An example of one of the worst cases of confusion is shown by the following program:

```
a is [x] { x+1 where x is 2 };
x is 3;
```

There are three possible Expressions that might be associated with the "x" in the Expression "x+1". Since syntactically the **where** clause is bracketed with "x+1" and then the Formal bracketed with the resultant Expression, it would seem most sensible if the "x" referred to was from the Definition in the **where** clause, and this is indeed the case. Thus by following the syntactic bracketing of the Program it is possible to resolve such confusion. It is only when a Name is defined more than once in a single list of Definitions that it is actually an illegal program. It should be noted that, although it is important to understand how some possible confusion is resolved, in writing programs it is much better to use distinct names so that the Program itself is clearer.

To summarize the situation, the scope of Names is as follows:

a) the scope of a Formal is the whole of the Expression that forms the body of the function specification;

b) the scope of a Name defined in an auxiliary Definition is the whole of the smallest Expression of which it forms a part.

Note that b) implies that Names from auxiliary Definitions are in scope in the Definitions at the same level; this also applies to Names defined at the top-most level of the Program.

Another source of problems in many languages is the question of whether the use of a Name in an Expression means the Name itself or the value to which that name refers. The distinction is meaningful in a language that has named memory cells (i.e. variables) because the value in a memory cell might change. In a language with no such changeable memory cells, such as SUGAR, it can be seen that the result of a program, if produced, will always be the same whether we either define new Names to replace Expressions or replace Names by the Expressions to which they refer. This is known as the principle of "referential transparency". For example, consider the following function:

```
real_roots is [a,b,c]
               { if   discriminant > 0
                 then < (−b + sqrt(discriminant)) / (2*a),
                        (−b − sqrt(discriminant)) / (2*a) >
                 elsf discriminant = 0
                 then { <repeated, repeated>
                        where repeated is −b/(2*a)
                        }
                 elsf discriminant < 0
                 then "error: imaginary roots"
                 endf
                 where discriminant is b*b − 4*a*c
               };
```

Various decisions have been made about what subdefinitions to make, mainly with the intention of making the program readable. It would have been quite reasonable to extract some more of the common subexpressions such as "2*a", and make these into subdefinitions, or we could have taken the opposite approach and replaced the names with the actual expressions to which they refer. Thus two further versions of the same function might be:

```
real_roots_1 is [a,b,c]
               { if   discriminant > 0
                 then { < (−b + square_root) / denominator,
                          (−b − square_root) / denominator >
                        where square_root is sqrt(discriminant)
                        }
                 elsf discriminant = 0
                 then { < repeated, repeated >
                        where repeated is −b / denominator
                        }
                 elsf discriminant < 0
                 then "error: imaginary roots"
                 endf
                 where discriminant is b*b − 4*a*c;
                       denominator is 2*a
               };

real_roots_2 is [a,b,c]
               if (b*b − 4*a*c) > 0
               then < (−b + sqrt(b*b − 4*a*c)) / (2*a),
                      (−b − sqrt(b*b − 4*a*c)) / (2*a) >
               elsf (b*b − 4*a*c) = 0
               then < (−b / (2*a)), (−b / (2*a)) >
               elsf (b*b − 4*a*c) < 0
               then "error: imaginary roots"
               endf;
```

The decision about which subexpressions to make into subdefinitions and which to leave in place is usually one of readability, but in practice there is often a further consideration to be borne in mind, and that is efficiency. Of course the programmer is not directly concerned with the actual method of execution of the program, but it might be reasonable to surmise that a function such as "real_roots_1" is likely to compute the expression "b*b − 4*a*c" less often than is "real_roots_2". In general the tendency is to make programs more readable by introducing subdefinitions, and so such possible in-efficiencies are not introduced, but it is useful to be aware of the possible problem.

EXERCISE

Determine the values of the following Expressions:

```
a)   { x + y where x is 3; y is 4 + x }
b)   ([x] x+1) (6)
c)   ([x] { x + y where x is 3; y is 4 + x } ) (6)
d)   < [n]n+1, [n]n, [n]n−1 > (2)
```

2.6 AN EXAMPLE

As a further example of the use of SUGAR we present a set of functions for dealing with matrices.

We represent a matrix as a list of rows, each row being in turn a list of elements. Thus we might have:

```
m1 is < <1,2,3>,
         <4,5,6>,
         <7,8,9>
       >;
m2 is < <1,0,0>,
         <0,1,0>,
         <0,0,1>
       >;
```

The first requirement is for a function to print out a matrix neatly since the response of the system to "m1?" is to print all the elements on one line with no spacing (i.e. "123456789"). The method used is to proceed down each list recursively, dealing with the first element of the list and then performing the same function on the rest of the list, adding spaces or newlines where appropriate. Such a technique is very common in dealing with lists in functional languages.

```
print is # the function that takes a matrix and
           prints it laid out on separate lines with
           spaces between the elements
         #
         [mat] { if    mat = <> then <>
                 else pr_row(hd mat) && nl : print(tl mat)
                 endf
                 where pr_row is [row]
                               if    row = <> then <>
                               else (hd row) : sp : pr_row(tl row)
                               endf
               };
```

In order to define the normal operations on matrices we must define functions that take the appropriate number of matrices as parameters, and deliver a new matrix. A similar method to that of print is used to specify the transpose and addition functions. Recall that the transpose of a matrix is found by reflecting the elements about the diagonal from the top left to the bottom right, and the sum of two matrices is the matrix where each element is the sum of the two corresponding elements of the operands. Finally, we show some requests for evaluation with their responses.

```
transpose is [m]
        { if    hd m = <> then <>
          else heads(m) : transpose(tails(m))
          endf
          where
            heads is [m] if m = <> then <>
                            else (hd (hd m)) : heads(tl m) endf;
            tails is [m] if m = <> then <>
                             else (tl (hd m)) : tails(tl m) endf
        };
add is [m,n]
        { if    m = <> or n = <> then <>
          else <add_row(hd m, hd n)> && add(tl m, tl n)
          endf
          where
            add_row is [r1,r2]
                    if    r1 = <> or r2 = <> then <>
                    else (hd r1)+(hd r2) : add_row(tl r1, tl r2)
                    endf
        };
```

```
print(m1)?
1  2  3
4  5  6
7  8  9

print(add(m1,m2))?
2  2  3
4  6  6
7  8  10

print(transpose(m1))?
1  4  7
2  5  8
3  6  9
```

EXERCISES

1. Recall that for matrix multiplication each element of the new matrix is found by summing the products of the associated row and column of the left and right operand matrices respectively. Thus, for example, if "m1" and "m2" are as above then "mult(m1,m2)(2,3)" is $(4*0 + 5*0 + 6*1)$ giving 6. Write the "mult" function.

2. Since SUGAR permits functions to be passed around as easily as lists, it would have been possible to allow the matrices to be represented as functions. Thus "transpose" could have been succinctly defined as:

```
transpose is [m] [x,y] m(y,x);
```

   a) Define the "add" function in the same way.
   b) Define the matrix with all elements zero.
   c) Define the general diagonal matrix.
   d) Given that all the matrices are 3x3, define a "print"
      function to work with these matrices.

2.7 ANOTHER EXAMPLE

The next example in this chapter is of a method of implementing a "turtle" to draw shapes on the screen under program control. The "turtle" function will be presented with a list of commands and cause the cursor to move about the screen depositing the characters in the appropriate places. Thus, for example, the request

```
turtle(<forward,forward,right,
        forward,forward,right,
        forward,forward,right,
        forward,forward>)?
```

will cause a small square to be printed. We shall assume that the user has a terminal that allows the cursor to be moved up, down, left and right. In addition, for the sake of neatness, we assume that the screen can be cleared, leaving the cursor at the top left hand corner. For the purposes of the program the characters that perform these functions will be known as "up_char", "down_char", "left_char", "right_char" and "clear_char".

The turtle is an interesting problem for a functional language for two reasons. Firstly, it is usually viewed very much in a procedural sense of "do this and then do this" and this contrasts strongly with the definitional view of functional programming. Secondly, we need to have some idea of the "state" of the turtle at a given place, for example which direction it is pointing in and what character is being drawn; this appears to be at variance with the idea of having no addressable, changeable memory in a functional language.

The way we approach this problem is to concentrate on the output and thus view the turtle function as defining the string of characters that perform the correct movements. So the top level specification is:

```
turtle is the function that takes a list of turtle functions
        that it knows how to perform as input and delivers
        the character string that draws the corresponding
        shape on the terminal
- - - - -
```

Each of the input functions will define a (possibly null) list of characters that correspond to the command. Functions will need to know the "state" of the turtle before they perform, and will also return the new state afterwards. It will thus be simplest if the function returns a pair representing the output string so far and the "state" of the turtle so far. The "turtle" function itself thus applies each of the functions in its input list in turn, making sure that the correct state is provided at each stage. (Such a function that takes functions as its parameters, or delivers a function as its result, is often termed a "higher order" function.)

```
turtle is # the function that takes a list of turtle functions
            that it knows how to perform as input and delivers
            the character string that draws the corresponding
            shape on the terminal
          #
    [commands]
      { moves(commands, initial_state)
      where
        moves is [commands, state]
          { if    commands = <> then ""
            else next(1) && moves(tl commands, next(2))
            endf
          where
            next is (hd commands)(state)
          }
      };
```

We now begin to define the turtle functions. The function "clear" is one of the simplest of the functions since it leaves the state unchanged and merely adds the "clear_char" string to the string so far.

```
clear is # the function that causes the turtle to clear
          the screen #
          [state] < <clear_char>, state >;
- - - - -
```

In order to define further functions we must decide exactly how we will represent the "state" of the turtle. In this example the "state" will be a list of two elements representing the current turtle character and the direction in which the turtle is pointing. The addition of further variations is left as an exercise. The direction of the turtle we will code as an integer from 1 to 4, according to whether the turtle is pointing north, east, south or west respectively. We also need to decide what the starting state will be; we will have the turtle drawing an asterisk and pointing east.

```
            initial_state is <'*, 2>;
```

Defining further functions to turn to the left and right and move forward are just slightly more complex variations of "clear":

```
left is [state] { < "", <state(1), new_direction> >
              where new_direction is <4,1,2,3>(state(2))
              };
right is [state] { < "", <state(1), new_direction> >
              where new_direction is <2,3,4,1>(state(2))
              };
forward is [state]
        { < move, state >
        where move is < up_char, right_char,
                       down_char, left_char > (state(2))
                    : state(1)
                    : <left_char>
        };
```

Finally, we define the function that changes the current character. This function must take not only the state as parameter but also the character to which it is required to change. Thus we must define a function such that when it is applied to a character parameter it delivers the required turtle function.

```
char is [ch] [state] < "", < ch, state(2) > >;
```

It is important to understand that the result of, for example, the expression "char('#)" is the function which takes a list of commands as a parameter and does certain turtle actions. In fact in SUGAR any function can have some of its parameters specified and then be passed around as a value before being finally applied. Thus "char" could equivalently have been defined as "char is [ch, state] {...". Such functions that are applied to their parameters one at a time are known as "curried" functions and we note that all functions in SUGAR are considered to be curried.

To finish this section, we show how to define the list that draws a 3x3 square by first defining the auxiliary function "many" that repeats a list of functions a specified number of times:

```
many is [comms, n] if   n = 0 then <>
                    else comms && many(comms, n-1)
                    endf;
square is many( many(<forward>,3) && <right>, 4 );
turtle(square)?
```

EXERCISES

1. Define the function "about_face" that turns the turtle around.

2. Define the function "move" that takes an integer parameter and moves the turtle forward that number of steps.

3. Extend the turtle program to include functions "pen_up" and "pen_down" that lift the pen up (so that it does not deposit characters) and down (so that it does).

4. Define the function to draw lines at an angle and then use it to define the function that draws a square rotated through 45 degrees.

2.8 YET MORE EXAMPLES

So far we have not assumed any particular evaluation mechanism for SUGAR. We mentioned earlier that SUGAR uses a mechanism called "lazy evaluation". Intuitively this means that each expression will only be evaluated if or when the result is needed (and in addition it will only be evaluated once). Using this mechanism enables us to define certain lists that could not be defined the same way if all specified expressions were evaluated.

As a small example consider the problem where the "nth" factorial number is required in a number of places. We could define factorial in the usual way:

```
fact is [n] if n = 1 then 1 else n * fact(n-1) endf;
```

Although this is an adequate solution, it may not always be the best: if, for example, we requested the evaluation of the expression "fact(100)" more than once, we can surmise that the value is recalculated each time. In SUGAR it is possible to define the list of all factorial numbers, safe in the knowledge that the system will only work out as much of the list as it needs. Of course if we ask for all the factorial numbers it will attempt to compute them, but this is the same behavior as the function above. We can thus define our infinite list of factorials as follows:

```
fac is 1 : { fac_from(2)
           where fac_from is [n] n * fac(n-1) : fac_from(n+1)
           };
```

This device of defining a small recursive function to compute the rest of the list is a common way of defining such infinite structures.

As another example of the definition of an infinite list we show the "Sieve of Eratosthenes" which is used to give the "nth" prime number. The idea of this method is that we start with the list of all the integers and filter out all multiples (starting from 2). We then notice that in fact it will only be necessary to filter out all multiples of prime numbers, since the multiples of any other integers will have been filtered out already. Thus first we define the list "primes" to be the sieve of the list of integers, and then we define "sieve" to be the list with the multiples filtered out:

```
primes is
    { sieve(from(2))
    where from is [n] n : from(n+1);
          sieve is [nums]
                hd nums : sieve(filter(hd nums, tl nums));
          filter is [num, list]
                    if   (hd list) rem num = 0
                    then filter(num, tl list)
                    else hd list : filter(num, tl list)
                    endf
    };
```

EXERCISE

The Fibonacci series is the list such that each element is the sum of the previous two, starting with two elements of 1 (i.e. 1 1 2 3 5 8 13 21 ...). Define the list whose elements are the Fibonacci series.

BIBLIOGRAPHY

The language SUGAR has been designed to provide consistency of notation with the previous functional programming languages, discussed in the references below. Landin is a seminal paper discussing ideas and issues in functional programming and Burge includes extensive examples of the use of a similar notation to SUGAR. Henderson looks at many applications using a design language similar to SUGAR.

[Bu1] Burge W.H. "Recursive Programming Techniques", Addison-Wesley, 1975.

[Hen] Henderson P. "Functional Programming: Application and Implementation", Prentice-Hall International, 1980.

[Lan] Landin P.J. "The Next 700 Programming Languages", Communications of the ACM, Vol. 9, pp. 157-166, March 1966.

PART 2

MATHEMATICAL FOUNDATIONS AND IMPLEMENTATION

Now that we have presented our programming methodology and the language SUGAR, the justification for some of the claims that we made for functional programming may be clearer. It is certainly true that functional programs are generally shorter than their imperative counterparts, making them easier to read and understand and thus to maintain. Another claim that we made was that, given the firm mathematical foundations of functional programming, it was easier to prove things about functional programs. In this part of the book we present the theoretical foundations of functional programming and discuss some of the techniques that may be used when implementing functional languages.

It is not possible to discuss the mathematical foundations of functional programming without a formal notation for function definition and application. The usual notation that is used in mathematical textbooks, although clear to the human reader, is not rigorous enough for our purposes. Fortunately, this problem has already been faced by logicians in the thirties and forties leading to several formal notations. In Chapter 3 we present the λ-calculus (read lambda-calculus), one such notation, and show how it models function definition and application in applicative languages.

The λ-calculus is used throughout the rest of this part of the book. It is a simple notation and yet is powerful enough to model all of the more esoteric features of functional languages. In Chapter 4, we discuss the parameter passing mechanisms that may be used in functional programming languages, relating this discussion to evaluation strategies used in the λ-calculus. We also present an interpreter for SUGAR that is written in SUGAR. This is suggestive of techniques that may be used to implement higher order functions and other features that are central to functional programming.

More effective implementation strategies are presented in Chapter 5, where we look at three different techniques. On conventional machines, functional languages are nearly always interpreted. This is because of a fundamental mismatch between the requirements of functional programming and the facilities offered by conventional machines. The classical interpretation mechanism is the SECD machine which is presented in Section 5.1. A more recent approach, the SK-reduction machine, which is based on a graphical representation for programs, is presented in the next section and, finally, we look to the future by discussing parallel implementations based on the data flow concept.

In the final chapter of this part of the book we return to the formal aspects of functional programming. We define the mathematical meaning (semantics) of SUGAR programs and show how the semantics may be used to prove properties of the programs.

3

THE λ-CALCULUS

We start this chapter with an informal description of the λ-calculus notation. The process of function application is modelled in the λ-calculus by a set of conversion rules that effectively tells us how to "simplify" an expression. The substitution that is performed by the rules is formally specified in Section 3.2 and the rules themselves are presented in Section 3.3. The first three sections refer to a pure λ-calculus. In the programming language context it is useful to define certain symbols in the notation to have special meanings, for example the integers and arithmetic operators. In the fourth section of this chapter we present such an "applied" λ-calculus and discuss the problems of fixed points and recursive definitions. Finally, it is possible to construct a complete arithmetic system using the pure calculus alone and approaches to this problem are presented in the fifth section.

3.1 AN INTUITIVE DEFINITION OF THE λ-CALCULUS

The basic symbols used in the λ-calculus are the variable names (drawn from an infinite set of possible names), λ, dot (.) and open and close brackets. In the rest of this chapter we use lower case alphabetic letters to represent variables. Upper case alphabetic letters are used to represent arbitrary expressions. The two main formation rules that we can use to construct expressions are the abstraction rule, used in the definition of functions, and the juxtaposition rule, used to represent a function application.

The general form for a function definition is shown below:

$$\lambda x . (M)$$

where M is an expression. (There are several alternative λ-calculus systems. The calculi differ in the constraints that are placed on the formation of the expression M. The calculus that we are going to use, which allows M to be any syntactically correct expression, is called the λK-calculus.) An example of a function definition is the identity function that is shown below:

$$\lambda x . (x)$$

The formation of a λ-expression from its component parts (x and M) is called abstraction or, more fully, functional abstraction. Some authors omit the brackets, when this does not give rise to any ambiguity, and we shall do this whenever possible. Thus the identity function above will normally be written:

$$\lambda x. x$$

Intuitively, the x represents the parameter to the function and the M defines what the function does with its parameter. It is of course possible to define functions with more than one parameter and this is done by nesting λ-expressions. We will normally use an alternative notation for such functions which involves a single λ followed by a list of parameters before the dot. The following function is an example of this notation:

$$\lambda x. (\lambda y. (x y))$$

which will be written: $\lambda xy. x y$

The variables between the lambda and the dot are formally called the bound variables of the λ-expression and the expression following the dot is called the body of the λ-expression. In a λ-expression that is composed of several subexpressions there may be some confusion about how far the body of a λ-expression extends. The convention is that the body of an expression extends as far to the right as is meaningful, which is normally the end of the whole expression or the first unmatched closing bracket.

Function application, as already intimated, is represented by juxtaposing one expression with another. Ambiguities can be resolved by the use of brackets. Function application associates to the left so that an expression like the one shown below:

f g h

is equivalent to:

(f g) h

not to:

f (g h)

as might have been expected from school mathematics. Another example of a function application is

(λ xy. x y) (λ z. z) w

Intuitively, it should be possible to simplify such an expression by substituting the "parameters" (λ z.z) and w, for the bound variables in the body of the "function" part of the application. Informally, a variable is bound in the body of a λ-expression if it appears in the bound variable list of the expression; a variable may also be free in an expression. Free variables are analogous to variables that have been inherited from an outer scope in an imperative program. If we can perform the substitution (Section 3.3 gives the formal rules for doing it) the expression may be simplified to:

(λ y. (λ z. z) y) w

and then to: (λ z. z) w

and this, finally, can be simplified to w. Unfortunately, we get into trouble if we apply this substitution process indiscriminately since we run the risk of introducing name clashes. For example, the following expression simplifies as shown:

(λ xy. x y) y

simplifies to: (λ y. y y)

and this has obscured the fact that the first occurrence of y in the body of the resultant expression is a totally different entity from the second y. A substitution rule that overcomes this problem by renaming one of the variables is specified in Section 3.2.

Once a subexpression has been simplified in this way, any other occurrences of the same subexpression within the expression may be replaced by the simplified form. This property of the λ-calculus, shared by functional programming languages, is the property of referential transparency as we noted in Chapter 2. Most expressions in imperative languages are not referentially transparent because their values depend on the current state of the machine, thus the same subexpression may have many different values (simplifications). The substitution rule tells us how to convert an expression from one form into another equivalent but simpler form. This notion of equivalence is formalized in the λ-calculus by the axiom of extensionality. The axiom states that two functions are equal if they have the same values for every possible set of parameter values.

We close this section with a summary of the notation that is involved in the λ-calculus. The summary takes the form of a definition of a valid λ-expression using our modified Backus Naur Form.

```
Expression ::= Variable_name |
               Expression Expression |
               λ Variable_name_list . Expression |
               ( Expression )
```

3.2 A SUBSTITUTION RULE

In this section we introduce a substitution rule that avoids the problem of name clashes. However, before we can present the substitution rule, we need to formalize the notion of bound and free variables. We can proceed by considering the definition of the last section and stating, for each alternative clause, what are the constraints for a variable to be bound (or free) in an expression of that type. Formally, the definition of free and bound occurrences of a variable x is as follows.

```
E1: The variable x occurs free in the expression x. No
    variable is bound in an expression consisting of a
    single variable.

E2: The variable x occurs free (or bound) in YZ if and
    only if it occurs free (or bound) in Y or Z.

E3: If the variable x does not occur in V then it occurs
    free (or bound) in λ V.Y if and only if it occurs
    free (or bound) in Y. All occurrences of the
    elements of V are bound in λ V.Y .
```

```
E4: The variable x occurs free (or bound) in ( Y ) if
    and only if it occurs free (or bound) in Y.
```

The definition is fairly self-explanatory. We must remember that bound variables are only introduced by functional abstraction. Thus any expression, such as a single variable, that does not contain any abstractions cannot contain any occurrences of bound variables. The use of brackets in the notation is either to resolve ambiguity or to enhance readability; in any case it can have no effect on the binding of variables in the bracketed expression. Within an abstraction, the bound variables of the abstraction are bound throughout the abstraction, otherwise, for any form of expression, variables occur bound or free depending on whether they occur bound or free in the constituent parts of the expression. The second clause of the definition allows both free and bound occurrences of a variable within the same expression. For example, in the expression shown below:

$$(\lambda y.y) y$$

the first and second occurrences of y are bound (by clause 3) but the third occurrence is free (by clauses 1 and 2).

We can now step through the specification of the substitution rule. First we introduce a formal notation for substitution, shown below, which can be read as "the expression formed when M replaces free occurrences of x in X". This process could introduce ambiguity so that it may be necessary to place parentheses around M during substitution in some circumstances.

$$[M / x] X$$

If X is a variable then the result of the substitution will be M or X depending on whether X is equivalent to x or not. Thus, using the case analysis technique, the first part of the rule is formally stated:

```
when X is the variable x then M
when X is a variable other than x then X            (3.1)
```

The rule for applications is also straightforward, we just substitute for x in each of the two immediate subcomponents of the application.

```
when X is the application Y Z then
              ( [ M / x ] Y ) ( [ M / x ] Z )       (3.2)
```

The definition of the rule for abstractions, which is where the possibility of name clashes arises, is presented below. The rule is clearer if we consider the longhand notation where all bound variables are immediately preceded by a λ.

```
when X is the abstraction λ x.Y then λ x.Y
when X is the abstraction λ y.Y and there are no free
  occurrences of x in Y then λ y.Y
when X is the abstraction λ y.Y and there are no free
  occurrences of y in M then λ y. [ M / x ] Y
when X is the abstraction λ y.Y and there is a free
  occurrence of y in M then λ z. [ M / x ] ( [ z / y ] Y )
              where z is a variable name that does not occur
              free in M or Y.
```

$$(3.3)$$

The first thing that this rule tells us is that if we encounter an abstraction, with a bound variable that is the same as the substitution variable, the binding of the abstraction takes precedence and protects the body from the effects of the substitution. This part of the rule applies to expressions such as:

```
  [ f / x ] ( x y ( λ x. x ) )
= ( [ f / x ] x ) ( [ f / x ] y ) ( [ f / x ] ( λ x. x ) )
                          by a double application of (3.2)
= f y ( λ x. x )          by a double application of (3.1)
                          and an application of (3.3)
```

From our informal description of the λ-calculus, it is clear that the occurrences of x in λx.x are different from the immediately preceding occurrence. The substitution rule conforms to this intuition. An analogous situation occurs in block-structured languages where an assignment to a variable does not affect the value of a variable of the same name that has been declared in an inner block.

If x does not occur free in Y then either it does not occur at all, or it is bound in an abstraction. In either case substituting for x will not have any effect on Y and this is what the first and second clauses of (3.3) tell us. Similarly if y is not free in M, it either does not appear at all in M or it is bound in an abstraction. When x does occur free in Y, as long as the constraint on y is satisfied, there can be no possibility of a name clash (substitution of a free occurrence of a variable into an expression where the variable is bound). Thus the third clause of (3.3) tells us that, in this situation, we can simply perform the substitution on the body of the abstraction. Finally, the last clause of (3.3) resolves the problem of name clashes. A name clash occurs when x is free in the body of the abstraction and y, the bound variable of the abstraction, occurs free in the expression that is to be substituted for x. The final clause tells us to change the name of the abstraction to the first available name that does not cause a further name clash. An example is shown below:

```
[ y / x ] λ y. x y
= λ z. [ y / x ] ( [ z / y ] x y )            by (3.3)
= λ z. [ y / x ] (([ z / y ] x ) ( [ z / y ] y ))   by (3.2)
= λ z. [ y / x ] ( x z )     by a double application of (3.1)
= λ z. (([ y / x ] x ) ( [ y / x ] z ))       by (3.2)
= λ z. y z              by a double application of (3.1)
```

which retains the meaning of the original expression (compare this with the example in Section 3.1).

Within the context of the substitution rule, brackets are not significant so that the expression [M / x] (Y) is clearly the same as ([M / x] Y).

Finally, to summarize this section we present the complete substitution rule.

```
[ M / x ] X is
when X is the variable x then M
when X is a variable other than x then X
when X is the application Y Z then
              ( [ M / x ] Y ) ( [ M / x ] Z )
when X is the abstraction λ x.Y then λ x.Y
when X is the abstraction λ y.Y and there are no free
 occurrences of x in Y then λ y.Y
when X is the abstraction λ y.Y and there are no free
 occurrences of y in M then λ y. [ M / x ] Y
when X is the abstraction λ y.Y and there is a free
 occurrence of y in M then λ z. [ M / x ] ( [ z / y ] Y )
              where z is a variable name that does not occur
              free in M or Y
otherwise  # X is ( Y ) #
              ( [ M / x ] Y ).
```

We now turn our attention to the simplification rules that can be applied to λ-expressions and investigate some of the implications of the substitution rule that is presented in this section.

EXERCISE

Perform the following substitutions:

a) [y / x] ((λ z. z x) (λ x. x))
b) [λ x. x y / x] ((λ y. x y) z)

3.3 THE CONVERSION RULES

The rules for simplifying λ-expressions are called conversion rules. There are three conversion rules, called α (alpha), β (beta) and η (eta). When an expression M is convertible with another expression N, using one of these rules, we write M cnv_a N (where a is the appropriate conversion rule). All of the conversion rules are reversible, and each rule states that wherever one of the expressions occurs it may be replaced by the other. The notation M cnv N is used to represent the fact that M is convertible with N using a series of conversion steps. The rules are presented below.

α : if there are no free occurrences of y in X
then   λ x. X cnv_α λ y. [y / x] X

β : (λ x. M) N cnv_β [N / x] M

η : if there are no free occurrences of x in M
then (λ x. M x) cnv_η M

The α rule tells us that, providing we do not introduce a name clash, we can freely change the bound variable names of an abstraction. This corresponds to our ability in programming languages to change the name of a formal parameter to a function, providing we do not change it to the same name as any of the local or global names used in the function. The β rule formalizes our earlier intuition about function application, and tells us that we can substitute actual parameters for formal parameters in an abstraction; alternatively it tells us that we can abstract subexpressions out of an expression. Finally the η rule says that one can remove, or introduce, levels of indirection in function applications. Given that there are no free occurrences of x in M, the following conversion applies:

(λ x. M x) N cnv_β [N / x] (M x) = M N

By applying the η rule first, we avoid the need to use the substitution rule.

An example of the use of the conversion rules is shown below:

$$(\lambda \, x. \, (\lambda \, yz. \, z \, y \,) \, x \,) \, p \, (\lambda \, x. \, x \,) \, cnv_\eta$$
$$(\lambda \, yz. \, z \, y \,) \, p \, (\lambda \, x. \, x \,) \, cnv_\beta$$
$$(\lambda \, z. \, z \, p \,) \, (\lambda \, x. \, x \,) \, cnv_\beta$$
$$(\lambda \, x. \, x \,) \, p \, cnv_\beta$$
$$p$$

Whereas the α rule does nothing to reduce the complexity of an expression, repeated applications of the other rules remove levels of abstraction when applied in a left-to-right direction, normally leading to an expression that cannot be simplified any further. However, this is not always the case. Consider the two examples shown below:

$$(\lambda \, x. \, x \, x \,) \, (\lambda \, x. \, x \, x \,) \quad cnv_\beta \quad (\lambda \, x. \, x \, x \,) \, (\lambda \, x. \, x \, x \,)$$

$$(\lambda \, x. \, x \, x \, x \,) \, (\lambda \, x. \, x \, x \, x \,)$$
$$cnv_\beta \, (\lambda \, x. \, x \, x \, x \,) \, (\lambda \, x. \, x \, x \, x \,) \, (\lambda \, x. \, x \, x \, x \,)$$
$$cnv_\beta \, (\lambda \, x. \, x \, x \, x \,) \, (\lambda \, x. \, x \, x \, x \,)$$
$$(\lambda \, x. \, x \, x \, x \,) \, (\lambda \, x. \, x \, x \, x \,)$$
.
.
.

In the first case the complexity does not change and in the second case it increases. In general, the simplifying property does apply to the expressions which we will be using. Because of this feature of the two rules they are sometimes called reduction rules, and instead of saying that an expression is convertible to another we say that it is reducible (written M red_a N where a is β or η ; M red N is used to represent the fact that M is reducible to N by a series of reductions and possibly some α-conversions). Analogously, some authors refer to right-to-left applications of the two rules as expansion rules; however we will not use this term further in the current text. An expression that can be reduced is called a redex ((λ x.M) N is a β-redex and λ x. M x is an η-redex).

An expression that contains no redexes is said to be in normal form. In some sense, the normal form of an expression is the value of that expression. It is not always possible to reduce an expression to a normal form; for example, the two expressions of the last example are not reducible. Given that a complex λ-expression may contain several candidate redexes there may be many possible reduction sequences that can be applied to an expression to reduce it to normal form. This raises the possibility that two different sequences of reductions may lead to different normal forms for the same expression. Fortunately, there is a theorem, the first Church Rosser Theorem, that guarantees that if an expression reduces to two normal forms they must be inter-convertible using an α-conversion. This theorem is formally stated below.

```
Church Rosser Theorem I :

    if X cnv Y
    then there exists an expression Z such that X red Z
        and Y red Z
```

We omit the proof of this theorem: the classical proof can be found in Curry and Feys [Cur] and is rather complex. A shorter, modern proof is reproduced in Barendregt [Bar]. The theorem does not, in itself, guarantee a unique normal form but the proof of our requirement follows quickly by a reductio ad absurdum proof.

```
Suppose that there are two distinct normal forms for an
expression A, say A red B and A red C (by distinct we
mean that they are not α-convertible).

Then C cnv A by our supposition (conversions are reversible)
and so C cnv B also by our supposition.

Therefore there is a Z such that C red Z and B red Z
(by the first Church Rosser Theorem).

But this is not possible because both B and C are normal
forms and thus do not contain any redexes.

Therefore our original supposition is wrong, i.e. no
expression can have two distinct normal forms.
```

If we reduce the redexes in an arbitrary order we may produce a non-terminating sequence of reductions, as in the two earlier examples. There is a second Church Rosser Theorem that tells us that if we always reduce the leftmost redex first, the reduction sequence will terminate with the normal form, if it exists. Before presenting the theorem we formally define the notion of leftmost redex:

```
If A and B are two redexes in an expression M and the first
occurrence of λ in A is to the left of the first occurrence
of λ in B then A is said to be TO THE LEFT OF B.

If A is a redex in M and it is to the left of all other
redexes then A is the LEFTMOST REDEX of M.
```

We now present the second Church Rosser Theorem:

```
Church Rosser Theorem II :

    if X red Y and Y is in normal form
    then there is a reduction sequence from X to Y
    which involves successively reducing the
    the leftmost redex
```

This order of reduction is called normal order reduction. Another possible order of reduction is applicative order which involves the reduction of the left and right subexpressions in an application before the application is reduced. Both approaches are of relevance in the programming language context as we shall see in Chapter 4.

Before we introduce a final example, we extend our notation by adding the ability to name λ-expressions. This is a powerful notational device that allows us to abbreviate long expressions by naming constituent subexpressions. By the property of referential transparency, a name is interchangeable with its defining expression and any expression that is convertible with it. The syntax for definitions is shown below.

```
Definition ::= Name = Expression
```

Unlike the convention that we have adopted for variable names, a Name in a Definition may be upper or lower case, and is not restricted to a single character.

We close this section by an example reduction sequence. In the following example we define the expressions S, K and I, sometimes called combinators. The term combinator is used to refer to a λ-expression that has no free variables in its body. We show how the λ-expression SKK is convertible to I using normal order reduction. (This example is based on an exercise in Stoy [Sto].)

```
S = λ xyz. x z ( y z )
K = λ xy. x
I = λ x. x

we want to show that SKK cnv I

SKK = ( λ xyz. xz ( yz ))( λ xy. x)( λ xy. x) cnv_β
      ( λ yz. ( λ xy. x) z ( yz ))( λ xy. x)  cnv_β
      λ z. ( λ xy. x) z ( ( λ xy. x) z)       cnv_β
      λ z. ( λ y. z) ( ( λ xy. x) z)          cnv_β
      λ z. z    cnv_α
      λ x. x
```

Combinators are dealt with in more detail in Chapter 5.

EXERCISES

1. Find the leftmost redex in the following expressions:

        (i) λ a. (λ b. bb) c ((λ d. d) a)
        (ii) (λ a. (λ yz. yz) a) (λ x. x) p

2. Given $B = \lambda xyz. x (yz)$ and S, K and I as defined above, show that S (KS) K cnv B.

3. Find the normal forms of the following expressions:

        (i) (λ x. ((λ z. zx) (λ x. x))) y
        (ii) (λ x. ((λ y. xy) z)) (λ x. xy)

3.4 RECURSIVE DEFINITIONS

The notation that we have presented so far is a purely formal system for manipulating symbols. In this section we introduce an extended calculus that forms a useful basis for the discussion of programming language concepts. The pure calculus that we have presented does not provide any convenient way of representing numbers, and operations on them, or definitions which involve choice, although we will illustrate how this may be done in the next section. We extend the calculus by adding numerical and logical constants, the basic arithmetic and logical operations and a conditional expression. Examples of the syntax are shown below; we define a "plus" function and a "maximum" function (that produces the maximum of its two arguments).

        plus = λ xy. x + y
        max = λ ab. if a > b then a else b

We can use conditional expressions to define recursive, or self-referential, expressions. An example of this technique is the Fibonacci function (where n is assumed to be greater than zero).

        f = λ n. if n < 3 then 1 else f(n−1) + f(n−2)

This is an equation in f. By the property of referential transparency, wherever the symbol f occurs it can be replaced by the expression on the right hand side of the equation. However, if we do this, we soon run into trouble because we get into a never-ending round of replacements (since f is recursive). So we must find a way of eliminating the recursion.

Before outlining a procedure for removing recursion from a definition, we must digress briefly and introduce the notion of a fixed point. The fixed points of a function are the set of values for which the function performs an identity transformation. This is restated differently and illustrated below.

```
The fixed points of f are the set of values, X, such that if x
is a member of X, then f(x) = x
```

```
e.g.
```

```
f = λ x. 6              X = { 6 }
f = λ x. 6 -- x         X = { 3 }
f = λ x. x*x + x - 4    X = { -2, 2 }
f = λ x. x              X = set of all values in the domain of f
f = λ x. x + 1          X = { }
```

As can be seen from the examples, a function may have one, many or no fixed points. How does this help us in eliminating recursion from equations like the definition of the Fibonacci function?

The first step is to abstract out the function name from the definition of the Fibonacci function.

```
F = λ gn. if n < 3 then 1 else g(n-1) + g(n-2)
```

We now notice that f, our original Fibonacci function, is a fixed point of F, as shown below.

```
Ff = ( λ gn. if n < 3 then 1 else g(n-1) + g(n-2)  ) f
   = λ n. if n < 3 then 1 else f(n-1) + f(n-2)
   = f
```

We proceed by hypothesizing the existence of a function Y that produces a fixed point for any arbitrary function. We can now rewrite the definition of f as a non-recursive equation.

```
f = Y F
```

This leaves us with the problem of how to define Y.

In Chapter 6 we will see that the formal semantics of functional programming languages guarantees that every function has at least one fixed point. Within this framework it is fairly easy to see that, given some function F, then a fixed point X of F is defined as below:

```
X = (λ x. F(xx)) (λ x. F(xx))

since   X cnv_β F((λ x. F(xx)) (λ x. F(xx)))
        =     F(X)
```

This immediately suggests that a general function Y, that can be used to find the fixed point of any function, can be defined as follows:

```
Y = λ h. ((λ x. h(xx)) (λ x. h(xx)))
```

Although this definition of Y follows easily from the definition of X, the reasons for choosing X in the first place may seem a bit mysterious. As it turns out, our choice of X does lead to the simplest definition of Y; however, there are many alternatives that we could have chosen. Another example is shown below:

```
X' = (λ xy. y(xxy)) (λ xy. y(xxy)) F

since   X' cnv_β λ y. (y((λ xy. y(xxy)) (λ xy. y(xxy)) y)) F
        cnv_β F((λ xy. y(xxy)) (λ xy. y(xxy)) F)
        = F(X')
```

The fixed point function derived from X' is shown below:

```
Y' = (λ xy. y(xxy))(λ xy. y(xxy))
```

The reader might have expected the F in the definition of X' to have been abstracted out of X' to produce Y' but, if we do that, the resultant expression is convertible with the definition given.

The class of fixed point operators is characterized by the following theorem, which is due to Böhm and is reproduced in Barendregt [Bar]:

```
Theorem :

Given the expression G = λ yf. f(yf), then M is a fixed
point operator if and only if M = GM.

Proof :

Part 1
      If M = GM
      Then for all F, MF = GMF
                         = (λ yf. f(yf)) M F
                         cnv F(MF)
      Therefore M is a fixed point operator
```

```
Part 2
    If M is a fixed point operator
    Then M cnv λ f. Mf
            = λ f. f(Mf)  since M is a fixed point operator
            cnv (λ yf. f(yf)) M
            = GM
```

Thus using this theorem we can confirm that Y is a fixed point operator:

```
Y = λ h. ((λ x. h(xx)) (λ x. h(xx)))
  cnv_β λ h. h((λ x. h(xx)) (λ x. h(xx)))
  cnv_β λ h. h((λ f. (λ x. f(xx))(λ x. f(xx))) h)
  = λ h. h(Yh)
  = GY
```

We conclude this section by illustrating, with three examples, how the fixed point function, Y, actually works. We start with a simple example:

```
let f = λ x. 6
then Y f = λ h.((λ x.h(xx))(λ x.h(xx))) (λ x. 6)
  cnv_β (λ x. (λ x. 6)(xx))(λ x.(λ x. 6)(xx))
  cnv_β (λ x. 6)((λ x.(λ x. 6)(xx))(λ x.(λ x. 6)(xx)))
  cnv_β 6
```

Next we show what happens when Y is applied to a function that appears not to have a fixed point:

```
let f = λ x. x + 1
then Yf = λ h. ((λ x.h(xx)) (λ x.h(xx))) (λ x. x+1)
  cnv_β (λ x. (λ x. x+1)(xx)) (λ x. (λ x. x+1)(xx))
  cnv_β (λ x. x+1)((λ x. (λ x. x+1)(xx))(λ x. (λ x. x+1)(xx)))
  cnv_β ((λ x. (λ x. x+1)(xx)) (λ x. (λ x. x+1)(xx))) + 1
  cnv_β λ h. ((λ x.h(xx)) (λ x.h(xx))) (λx. x+1) + 1
  = Yf + 1
```

Although this result appears to suggest that the fixed point does not exist, the formal semantics provides us with a special value (bottom) that satisfies this equation. (The reader must wait until Chapter 6 to find out more about this.)

The final example is to find the fixed point of the non-recursive Fibonacci function. Remember that the fixed point of this function is itself a function. It is easier to understand the mechanism if we actually apply the resultant function. Below, we illustrate this for the third Fibonacci number.

```
f(3)  = Y  F  3
cnv   λ h.(( λ x.h(xx))( λ x.h(xx))) F 3
cnv   ( λ x.F(xx))( λ x.F(xx)) 3
      let k = ( λ x.F(xx))
cnv   ( λ xgn.((if n<3 then 1 else g(n-1)+g(n-2))(xx))) k 3
cnv   ( λ gn.(if n<3 then 1 else g(n-1)+g(n-2)) (kk)) 3
cnv   ( λ n.(if n<3 then 1 else (kk)(n-1)+(kk)(n-2))) 3
cnv   (kk) 2 + (kk) 1
      (kk)2 and (kk)1 have similar reductions, so
      we concentrate on (kk)2
(kk)2 = ( λ x.F(xx)) k 2
cnv   ( λ xgn.((if n<3 then 1 else g(n-1)+g(n-2))(xx))) k 2
cnv   ( λ gn.((if n<3 then 1 else g(n-1)+g(n-2))(kk))) 2
cnv   ( λ n.(if n<3 then 1 else (kk)(n-1)+(kk)(n-2))) 2
cnv   1
also  (kk)1 cnv 1
thus  Y F 3 cnv 1 + 1 = 2 which is the third Fibonacci number
```

We return to the notion of fixed points and the Y function in Chapters 5 and 6.

EXERCISES

1. Show that Y′ is a fixed point operator.

2. (due to Klop and reproduced in Barendregt [Bar]) Given:

`# = λ abcdefghijklmnopqstuvwxyzr.r(thisisafixedpointcombinator)`

and   `$ = #########################`

show that $ is a fixed point operator.

3. Define a non-recursive factorial function in the extended λ-calculus. Illustrate how this works for the value 3.

3.5 ARITHMETIC IN THE PURE λ-CALCULUS

We suggested in the last section that there was no convenient way of representing the integers in the pure λ-calculus. While this is true to a large extent, several numeral systems have been devised and we present some of these in this section. The fact that we can define numeral systems along with their associated arithmetic operators illustrates the power of the pure λ-calculus as a model of computation. It can be shown that any function over the natural numbers may be constructed from a small set of primitive functions and a conditional construct. In fact, once we have defined the function's successor (increment), predecessor (decrement), "test if zero" and a fixed point operator we can go on to define any other function. (This notion is based on results from Recursive Function Theory; for example, see Minsky [Min].) In the rest of this section we introduce a representation for the numerals and show how the three new functions may be defined.

Firstly, we must define the two logical constants (true and false) and a conditional construct. The conditional can be defined as shown below:

```
if P then M else N  is defined as  (λ pmn. pmn) PMN
```

Of course, we expect P to be either true or false and also that the expression should produce M in the first instance and N in the second. This suggests that suitable representations for true and false are as shown below:

```
T = λ xy. x
          since    if T then M else N
                   = (λ pmn. pmn) TMN
                   cnv TMN
                   = (λ xy. x) MN
                   cnv M

F = λ xy. y
          since    if F then M else N
                   cnv FMN
                   cnv N
```

It is now possible to define a set of logical operations; for example, the "and" operation may be defined as shown below:

```
and = λ xy. xyF
```

```
and TT   cnv   TTF   cnv   T
and TF   cnv   TFF   cnv   F
and FT   cnv   FTF   cnv   F
and FF   cnv   FFF   cnv   F
```

The numerals will be defined recursively and thus any particular numeral may be considered to be a pair. The first element of the pair is the most significant "digit" and the second element is the rest of the numeral (in fact the predecessor of the numeral under consideration — so it might well be another pair). This representation has been chosen because it facilitates the definition of the primitive functions: an alternative notation will be presented later. We shall see that there are obvious similarities between these notations and the unary notation used in other formal systems such as Turing Machines. Before defining the numerals, we must introduce a notation for a pair of expressions:

```
[M,N] = λ z. zMN

first = λ x. xT
            since first [M,N]   cnv   TMN   cnv   M

second = λ x. xF
            since second [M,N]   cnv   FMN   cnv   N
```

We can now define the numerals:

```
0 = λ x. x = I
n + 1 = [F,n]    for all n >= 0

for example:
    3 = [F,[F,[F,I]]]
```

This definition immediately suggests a definition for the successor function:

```
succ = λ x. [F,x]

for example:
    succ 2 = succ [F,[F,I]]
                  cnv [F,[F,[F,I]]] = 3
```

The predecessor of any numeral is the second element of the pair that represents the numeral:

```
pred = second
```

```
for example:
    pred 3 = pred [F,[F,[F,I]]]
             cnv [F,[F,I]] = 2
```

Finally the "test if zero" function must produce T if applied to zero and F, which is the first element of any numeral pair, otherwise. Since the numeral 0 is the identity function, "first 0" is T and thus we can use the "first" function for the test:

```
ifzero = first

for example:
    ifzero 0  =  ifzero I  cnv  IT   cnv  T
    ifzero 1  =  ifzero [F,I]  cnv  [F,I] T  cnv  TFI  cnv  F
```

We could now go on to define all of the usual arithmetic operations; for example, the plus function is defined as shown below:

```
plus = Y λ fxy. if ifzero x then y else f (pred x) (succ y)
```

For further examples the reader is referred to the exercises. A more formal treatment of this notation may be found in Barendregt [Bar].

There are many other notations that have been devised. A classical example is the system proposed by Church [Chu] in which the numerals are defined as shown below:

```
0 = λ fx. x
n = λ fx. fⁿx      for all n > 0

for example:
    3 = λ fx. f(f(fx))
```

This system has the advantage that certain functions are very easy to define; for example, the multiplication function:

```
mult = λ xy. compose x y
       where compose = λ xyz. x(yz)

for example:
    mult 2 3  cnv   compose 2 3
              cnv   λ z. 2(3z)
              cnv   λ z. (λ fx. f(fx)) (3z)
              cnv   λ z. λ x. (3z)((3z)x)
              cnv   λ zx. (λ x. z(z(zx))) ((3z)x)
              cnv   λ zx. z(z(z((3z)x)))
              cnv   λ zx. z(z(z(z(z(zx)))))
              =  6
```

However, the definitions of the primitive functions are less straightforward than in the earlier notation.

Not surprisingly, all of the numeral systems are equivalent and we close this section with the definition of a mapping from our earlier notation to the Church notation. This definition uses a successor function for Church numerals; the definitions of this, the other primitive functions and the inverse mapping are left as an exercise.

```
tochurch = Y λ fx. if ifzero x then λ fx. x
                    else churchsucc(f (pred x))
```

EXERCISES

1. Define the logical functions "not" and "or".

2. Define multiplication and subtraction in the first numeral system.

3. Define the function "fromchurch", the inverse of "tochurch".

4. Define "succ", "pred" and "ifzero" for Church numerals.
(Hint: you may find "fromchurch" and "tochurch" useful.)

BIBLIOGRAPHY

Detailed and formal treatments of the λ-calculus can be found in Barendregt, in Church and in Curry and Feys. The Church Rosser Theorems and their proofs form a substantial part of Curry and Feys and a more modern, shorter proof of the first theorem is to be found in Barendregt. Stoy uses the λ-calculus as a vehicle for discussing some aspects of denotational semantics and presents a good introduction to the subject. Less detailed introductions to the λ-calculus may be found in Burge and Wegner. A survey of Recursive Function Theory is presented in Minsky.

[Bar] Barendregt H.P. "The Lambda Calculus — Its Syntax and
            Semantics", North-Holland, 1981.

[Bu1] Burge W.H. "Recursive Programming Techniques", Addison-

Wesley, 1975.

[Chu] Church A. "The Calculi of Lambda-Conversion", Annals of Mathematics Studies No. 6, Princeton University Press, 1941.

[Cur] Curry H.B. and Feys R. "Combinatory Logic, Volume 1", North-Holland, 1968.

[Min] Minsky M.L. "Computation : Finite and Infinite Machines", Prentice-Hall, 1967.

[Sto] Stoy J.E. "Denotational Semantics: The Scott-Strachey Approach to Programming Language Theory", MIT Press, 1977.

[Weg] Wegner P. "Programming Languages, Information Structures and Machine Organisation", McGraw-Hill, 1971.

4

INTERPRETATION OF FUNCTIONAL PROGRAMS

In the last chapter we suggested that an application of the β-reduction rule to a λ-expression is analogous to the notion of parameter passing in programming languages. In our discussion of the Church Rosser Theorems, we saw that the order of reduction could have important consequences for the evaluation of a λ-expression. Similar considerations arise in the programming language context. In the first part of this chapter, we discuss some of the options that are available to the language designer. In particular, we introduce the call-by-value, call-by-name and lazy evaluation parameter passing mechanisms.

The rest of the chapter is devoted to the description of an interpreter for SUGAR. The interpreter is written in SUGAR itself. An interpreter of this type (written in the language that it interprets) is sometimes called a meta-circular interpreter. This technique was first introduced by McCarthy et al. [McC] in the description of the LISP run-time system. A meta-circular interpreter serves to clarify some of the issues faced by the implementor; for example, how higher order functions should be handled. However, we should beware of treating the interpreter as though it specified an operational semantics for the language, since for detailed semantic questions it just reinforces our misunderstandings. If we have any misconceptions about the language the interpreter merely perpetuates these by defining basic notions in terms of themselves.

The interpreter executes a function that has already been converted into an internal form. The internal form is described in Section 4.2 and bears a superficial similarity to LISP (see Chapter 7). Section 4.3 describes informally how the interpreter works and the final section presents the design of the SUGAR interpreter program.

4.1 PARAMETER EVALUATION

In Chapter 3 we mentioned two alternative strategies (applicative order evaluation and normal order evaluation) that one can adopt when evaluating a λ-expression. Not surprisingly, the designer of a functional language is faced with a comparable choice of parameter passing mechanisms. We discuss the options below: both approaches have their drawbacks and thus we also introduce the concept of lazy evaluation which retains the advantages of both while avoiding their pitfalls. There are other mechanisms that are used in imperative languages (for example, call-by-result and call-by-reference) but, as they rely on global state changes, they are not considered relevant to functional languages. The reader who is interested in a more general treatment of parameter passing mechanisms is referred to the bibliographic notes at the end of this chapter.

Applicative order evaluation requires that the arguments to an application should be evaluated before they are passed to the function. In the programming language context this approach is called the call-by-value mechanism. PASCAL uses call-by-value parameter passing as one of its basic mechanisms. The parameters are evaluated and the values are stored in locations that are local to the function or procedure. Thus if we have a section of program as follows:

```
1       function sqrt ( x : integer ) : real ;
2       (*produce an approximation of the square root
3         of the parameter*)
4       var old, approx : real;
5       begin
6         approx := x / 2;
7         repeat
8           old := approx;
9           approx := ( old + x / old ) / 2
10          until abs ( approx - old ) < 0.000001;
11          sqrt := approx
12      end;
              .
              .
              .
13      i := 12;
14      j := 11;
              .
              .
15      (* call of function *)
16      h := sqrt ( i * j );
```

the function body that is actually executed at line 16 would effectively be as shown below.

```
            .
            .
            .
6           approx := 132 / 2;
7           repeat
8             old := approx;
9             approx := ( old + 132 / old ) / 2;
            .
            .
            .
```

The major advantage of the call-by-value mechanism is that the parameter is only evaluated once. The first data flow implementation of Chapter 5 uses this mechanism. A major disadvantage of the approach is that if one of the parameters to a function is undefined, or leads to a non-terminating computation, then the interpreter/machine will not terminate with a meaningful result. An example from the λ-calculus illustrates the problem:

$$(\lambda x y. 3 + y) ((\lambda x. x x) (\lambda x. x x)) 6$$

It would be reasonable to require the evaluation of the expression to deliver the value 9 because only the second "parameter" is used in the body. However, if we use applicative order evaluation, an evaluation of the expression will never terminate because the expansion of the first parameter is non-terminating.

Normal order evaluation avoids the above problem by passing the arguments before they are evaluated. The parameters are thus evaluated where they are needed (this may be in several places). Using normal order evaluation the expression above would have the value 9 as expected. Normal order evaluation is called call-by-name in programming language theory. PASCAL does not support the call-by-name mechanism, but if it did, we would effectively execute the function shown below for the earlier example.

```
            .
            .
            .
6           approx := ( i * j ) / 2;
7           repeat
8             old := approx;
9             approx := ( old + ( i * j ) / old ) / 2;
            .
            .
            .
```

In an imperative language the value of a parameter might change because of side-effects and thus different references to the parameter can have different values. The controlled use of this type of side effect is the basis of Jensen's device which is discussed in Ledgard and Marcotty [Led]. However, in a functional language the parameter always re-evaluates to the same value because there are no side-effects. Thus the use of call-by-name in functional languages would appear to be inefficient. However, our definition of the mechanism does allow for the parameter not to be evaluated if it is not required and thus certain computations will terminate successfully in a call-by-name system whereas they would not have done in a call-by-value system (as with our earlier example).

The lazy evaluation mechanism attempts to combine the advantages of both of the previous techniques. The parameters are passed using call-by-name but, once a parameter has been evaluated, its value is remembered (effectively turning it into a call-by-value parameter). For example, given the following SUGAR definition and application:

```
incl_or is [a,b] if a then a else b endf;

incl_or(true,incl_or(false,true))?
```

the first parameter of the application would be evaluated once and the second would not be evaluated at all because SUGAR uses lazy evaluation. The definition of lazy evaluation that we have given above corresponds to call-by-need parameter passing. However, there is an important difference in that if the parameter has a structured value, only the parts of the structure that are actually referred to are evaluated. Thus after the following definition and application:

```
from is [n] n : from(n+1);

hd(tl from(1))?
```

only the first two elements of the infinite list from(1) will have been evaluated. The SK-reduction machine provides a lazy evaluation parameter passing mechanism. Also some data flow (demand-driven) systems provide lazy evaluation.

We now turn our attention to the meta-circular interpreter for SUGAR.

EXERCISES

1. What would the value of

```
hd(tl from(1))
```

be in a system that uses call-by-value parameter passing?

2. Parameters may contain free-variables, for example:

```
incl_or(false,a)
```

What problems does this cause in a system that uses call-by-name parameter passing? Suggest a solution to the problem. (We deal with this problem in Section 4.3.)

4.2 AN INTERNAL FORM FOR SUGAR

The interpreter presented in the next few sections requires that SUGAR functions should be represented as lists of symbols in an internal form. It would be possible to write parsing routines to convert SUGAR to this internal form; however, this would obscure the workings of the interpreter and so is left as an exercise for the reader.

Before discussing the internal form in detail, we present a definition of its syntax. The angle brackets, double quote (″) and comma (,) are reserved as constant symbols that have their usual SUGAR meanings. The separator for lists is comma (,).

```
Internal_form ::=
            Constant |
            "name" |
            < "name", Internal_form_list > |
            < Cond_op, Clause_list > |
            < Lambda_op,< Internal_form_list >,Internal_form > |
            < Label_op, "name", Internal_form > |
            < Funarg_op, Internal_form, < Association_list >>
Clause ::= < Internal_form, Internal_form >
Association ::= < "name", Internal_form >
```

The syntax is discussed in detail and the interpreter operators (such as "Cond_op") are defined in the following sub sections. We postpone the discussion of "Funarg_op" until Section 4.3.

4.2.1 Constants

This category includes the integers, real numbers, truth values and single character constants. Constants are represented by themselves in the internal form.

4.2.2 Bound Variable and Function Names

Bound variable and function names are converted into strings in the internal form.

```
x becomes "x"

boundv1 becomes "boundv1"
```

4.2.3 Function Applications

A function application is represented by a list. The first element of the list is the name of the function which is being applied. This function may be a primitive function or a user-defined function. The rest of the list is constructed from the appropriately converted parameters of the application.

The primitive functions are the operators that are built into the interpreter. The operators are converted into upper case character strings that represent the appropriate primitive functions. An example of the application of a primitive function is shown below:

```
x + 1 becomes < "PLUS", "x", 1 >
```

As an example of a user-defined function application, assume that a maximum function (max) that takes two parameters and returns the maximum of the two values has been defined by the user:

```
max ( x * y, 1 )

becomes  < "max", < "TIMES", "x", "y" >, 1>
```

4.2.4 Conditional Expressions

A conditional expression is converted into a list whose first element is the conditional operator ("COND"). Each element of the rest of the list is a list that corresponds to one of the clauses of the conditional. The first element of each list is the appropriately converted condition and the second element is the converted then-expression. The else-clause is treated as though it were an elsf-clause with a true condition. This is illustrated below.

```
if n = 0 then 1
else n * fac ( n - 1 )
endf
```

becomes

```
< "COND", << "EQZERO", "n" >, 1>,
          < true,< "TIMES", "n", <"fac",< "PRED", "n">>>>
>
```

4.2.5 Unnamed Function Definitions

In this category we include all expressions that consist of a bound variable list followed by a function body. The definition is converted into a list whose first element is the lambda operator ("LAMBDA"), the second element is a list of converted bound variable names and the third element is the converted body:

```
[ x, y ] x * x + y * y
```

becomes

```
< "LAMBDA", < "x", "y" >,
   < "PLUS", < "TIMES", "x", "x" >, < "TIMES", "y", "y" >>
>
```

4.2.6 Named Function Definitions

Finally, we introduce the transformation for named function definitions. This category includes all functions that are defined by SUGAR definition statements. The definition is converted to a list of three elements. The first element is the label operator ("LABEL"), the second is the function name and the third element is a converted definition body (an unnamed function definition). The "max" function, that finds the maximum of its two arguments, is converted as follows.

```
max is [ a, b ] if a > b then a
                else b
                endf
```

becomes

```
< "LABEL", "max",
   < "LAMBDA", < "a", "b" >,
      < "COND", << "GT", "a", "b" >, "a" >,
                  < true, "b" >
      >
   >
>
```

The transformations that have been discussed will allow us to translate any SUGAR function except those that use lists or higher order functions or rely on auxiliary definitions. Higher order functions and auxiliary definitions are discussed in the next section. Exercise 2 invites the reader to consider support for lists within the interpreter.

EXERCISES

1. Convert the following SUGAR functions into the interpreter's internal form:

```
(i) f is [a,b] a — b * b;

(ii) fib is [n] if n = 1 then 1
              elsf n = 2 then 1
              else fib(n—1) + fib(n—2) endf;
```

2. Enhance the syntax of Internal form to support lists and define a scheme for translating SUGAR lists into your internal form.

4.3 THE BASIC INTERPRETATION MECHANISM

The interpreter expects to be passed a SUGAR function and a list of arguments. The SUGAR function may be a primitive function, an unnamed function, a labelled function or a function closure (which is described later). Parameters are evaluated before being passed to the function. This would appear to correspond to the call-by-value mechanism but the reader is referred to the end of Section 4.4 for a discussion of this.

The interpreter maintains an association list, or environment, which consists of a pair for each name that is currently known to the interpreter. The pair is a list whose first element is the name and whose second element is the associated value. For example, the SUGAR program to add all numbers from a value less than ten up to ten might be executed as shown below and, during the interpretation of the first application of "sum10", the association list would be as shown.

```
sum10 is [ n ] if n = 10 then 10
                else n + sum10 ( n + 1 )
                endf ;
```

an interpreter call might be:

```
interpret( <"LABEL", "sum10",
            <"LAMBDA", <"n">,
             <"COND",<<"EQ","n",10>,10>,
               <true,<"PLUS","n",<"sum10",<"PLUS","n",1>>>>
             >
             >
           >,<1>)?
```

and the association list is:

```
<< "n", 1>,
 < "sum10", < "LAMBDA", < "n" >, < "COND" ... >>>,
 >
```

As we noted at the end of the last section, the internal form will not allow us to interpret functions which produce functions as results. The reason for this problem (sometimes called the FUNARG problem) is that the resultant function may contain free variables that are bound within the producing function but are no longer bound when the resultant function is applied. A SUGAR example of the problem might be:

```
add is [ a, b ] a + b;
add1 is add ( 1 );
sum is [ a ] add1 ( a );
```

At the time that the function "add1" is produced the bound variable "a" is associated with the value 1. However, when "add1" is applied, "a" is associated with the value of the actual parameter of "sum". The solution that we adopt is simply to remember the environment that was extant at the time that the function "add1" was created. This is done by causing the value of the call to "add" with one parameter to be a function closure which consists of the function body along with the associated environment. In our internal form the function closures are represented by a list which consists of the operator "FUNARG", followed by the function body, followed by the associated environment. The function closure that the second line in our example would produce is shown below.

$$<"FUNARG", <"LAMBDA", <"b">, <"PLUS", "a", "b">>, <<"a", 1>>>$$

In order to force the production of a closure, we require that higher order functions are explicitly represented by nested "LAMBDA" expressions. Thus "add" should be converted to its curried form:

$$<"LAMBDA", <"a">, <"LAMBDA", <"b">, <"PLUS", "a", "b">>>$$

The other problem that was mentioned in the last section was that of incorporating auxiliary function definitions into the interpretation mechanism. The approach taken in many interpreters is that auxiliary definitions are introduced in a list whose first element is the operator "DEFINE". The effect of the define operator is that the functions that follow are added to the association list where they may be found when the main function is evaluated. The extensions to the interpreter are left as an exercise for the reader.

EXERCISE

Design a notation that may be used to represent auxiliary definitions in the internal form and translate an example using your notation.

4.4 THE INTERPRETER

The interpreter takes two parameters, an expression and a list of arguments. The expression is applied to the arguments. It will be remembered from the last section that expressions can only be evaluated relative to some particular environment. When the interpreter is called there are initially no entries in the association list, so the expression is applied to its arguments using an empty environment. The interpret function can be described as follows:

```
interpret is the function with parameters exp and arg-list
which applies the exp to the arg-list using an empty
association list
```

This definition implies the need for a three parameter function which we shall call "apply" and which must be capable of handling constants, primitive functions, user-defined function names, unnamed function definitions, named function definitions and function closures. The design of the apply function is shown below.

```
apply is the function with parameters exp, arg-list and
    environment which
when the exp is a constant delivers the constant,
when the exp is a primitive operator then computes the result
    of applying the operator to the evaluated arguments,
when the exp starts with a lambda operator then evaluates
    the lambda body in the environment prefixed with
    appropriate bound variable/evaluated arg pairs,
when the exp starts with a label operator then applies the
    unnamed function definition part to the args in an
    environment that has been prefixed by a pair associating
    the label name with the unnamed function definition,
when the exp is a function closure then applies the function
    body to the args in the environment specified
    by the closure,
otherwise applies the evaluated exp to the args using the
    current environment
```

Thus with unnamed function definitions, the bound variables are associated with the argument values and the function body is evaluated in this context. The label operator causes an entry to be added to the front of the association list tying the label name to the unnamed function definition that forms the second operand of the label operator. The function part of a function closure is applied to the arguments using the association list defined in the closure. Finally, user-defined function names are looked up in the association list and the appropriate function definition is applied to the arguments.

Several further functions are required by this definition. Notably we need a function that pairs bound variable names with argument values and adds them to the association list, a function to apply primitive operators and a function that evaluates expressions in the appropriate environment. The primitive application and pairing functions are trivial and their SUGAR definitions may be studied in the program at the end of this chapter. Studying the design of the apply function, we see that the evaluate function, "eval", must be able to evaluate anything that can form the body part of a lambda operator, any valid argument for primitive operators and any user-defined names. Thus it must handle conditionals, applications of primitive and user-defined functions, function producing expressions, constants and user-defined names. The design of eval is shown below.

```
eval is the function with parameters exp and environment which
when the exp is a constant or a name then produces the value
     of the exp from the association list,
when the exp is a conditional then evaluates the first
     expression whose evaluated case is true,
when the exp is an application of a primitive function (i.e. it
     starts with the function name) then applies the primitive
     function to the operands using the environment,
when the exp starts with the "LAMBDA" operator then produces a
     closure consisting of the exp and the current environment,
otherwise applies the head of the exp (a function) to its
     operands (the rest of the exp) using the environment
```

This function also needs some further function definitions. These include a function to evaluate the pairs in a conditional list ("evcon") and a function to look up names in the association list ("assoc"). As these functions are fairly trivial and introduce no new concepts they are shown only in their SUGAR form:

```
interpret is [f,x] { apply(f,x,<>)
  where
    apply is [f,x,a] {
    if atom f then f
    elsf prim(f) then app_prim(f,x,a)
    elsf hd f = "LAMBDA" then eval(f(3),pl(f(2),el(x,a),a))
    elsf hd f = "LABEL" then apply(f(3),x,<f(2),f(3)>:a)
    elsf hd f = "FUNARG" then apply(f(2),x,f(3))
    else apply(eval(f,a),x,a) endf
    where
      pl is [x,y,a] if x = <> then a
             else <x(1),y(1)>:pl(tl x,tl y,a) endf;
      eval is [e,a] {
        if (atom e) or (atom (hd e)) then assoc(e,a)
        elsf hd e = "COND" then evcon(tl e,a)
        elsf prim(hd e) then app_prim(e(1),tl e,a)
        elsf hd e = "LAMBDA" then <"FUNARG",e,a>
        else apply(hd e,tl e,a)
        endf
        where
         evcon is [c,a] if eval(c(1,1),a)
                        then eval(c(1,2),a)
                        else evcon(tl c,a)
                        endf;
```

```
                assoc is [x,a] if a = <> then x
                               elsf x = a(1,1) then a(1,2)
                               else assoc(x,tl a)
                               endf
          };
     el is [m,a] if m = <> then <>
            else eval(hd m,a) : el(tl m,a)
            endf;
     prim is [x] x = "EQ" or x = "PLUS" or x = "TIMES" ...;
     app_prim is [f,x,a] if f = "EQ"
                         then eval(x(1),a) = eval(x(2),a)
                         elsf f = "PLUS"
                         then eval(x(1),a) + eval(x(2),a)
                         elsf f = "TIMES"
                         then eval(x(1),a) * eval(x(2),a)
                                   .
                                   .
                                   .
                         endf
     }
};
```

We have written the interpreter so that it appears to use the call-by-value parameter passing mechanism. However, if it is run on a system that uses lazy evaluation, although the interpreter appears to be forcing evaluation, parameters will not be evaluated until they are required. It is important that the calls to "eval" and "el" are left in because they ensure that the right association list is used when the parameters are eventually evaluated.

That completes our description of the meta-circular interpreter. The simplicity of the program underlines the elegance of the functional approach.

EXERCISES

1. Enhance the interpreter so that it will accept auxiliary definitions.

2. Implement SUGAR lists and the associated operators in the interpreter.

3. Translate the following function to internal form:

```
        inc is [n] n + 1;
```

and trace what the interpret function does for the application:

```
inc(3) ?
```

(See Section 2.4 for information about program tracing.)

BIBLIOGRAPHY

There have been several books published recently about concepts used in programming languages. The two cited here both include sections on parameter passing mechanisms (Ledgard pp. 204 - 209; Tennent pp. 117 - 126). Henderson includes some discussion of parameter passing techniques for functional languages. A meta-circular interpreter for a functional language was first presented in McCarthy et al. and is also discussed in Henderson.

[Hen] Henderson P. "Functional Programming: Application and Implementation", Prentice-Hall International, 1980.

[Led] Ledgard H. and Marcotty M. "The Programming Language Landscape", Science Research Associates, 1981.

[McC] McCarthy J., Abrahams P.W., Edwards D.J., Hart T.P. and Levin M.I. "LISP 1.5 Programmer's Manual", MIT Press, 1962.

[Tel] Tennent R.D. "Principles of Programming Languages", Prentice-Hall International, 1981.

5

OTHER IMPLEMENTATIONS

In this chapter we are going to discuss three other ways of implementing functional languages. The first approach is suggestive of a machine for executing functional programs, the second two are less feasible at the moment, because of technological considerations, but may soon become viable bases for commercial architecture designs.

In Section 5.1 we describe the SECD machine. It is presented as a software interpreter but the implications for hardware design are fairly obvious. The SECD machine has become a standard way to implement functional programming languages in the twenty years since it was first invented. It uses a call-by-value mechanism for parameter passing but later extensions to the basic machine have been directed towards the support of a lazy evaluation mechanism (see Chapter 4). After a thorough discussion of the basic machine we show how it can be extended in this way.

The second approach is based on the use of combinators, which were briefly introduced in Chapter 3, and was initially described by David Turner in relation to his implementation of SASL. The system is described in Section 5.2. We show how a functional expression can be translated to variable-free combinator code and describe the SK-reduction machine that executes this code. Turner's machine is implemented in software at the moment although work is being done on hardware implementations, and a prototype has been built at the University of Cambridge.

Finally, in Section 5.3 we describe how functional languages might be implemented on data flow machines. Data flow is an approach to parallel processing that has received a lot of interest over the past five years. The work has close affinities with the basic philosophy of functional programming. However as there is still diversity of opinion about the nature of data flow, we present our own data flow notation and restrict ourselves to general comments about the architecture of data flow machines.

5.1 THE SECD MACHINE

The SECD machine has become the standard way to implement functional programming languages. It is based on an automaton designed by Peter Landin in the early sixties for mechanically evaluating mathematical expressions. Naturally, this work involved Landin in an investigation of mechanisms for function application and definition and, as we saw in Chapter 3, the λ-calculus provides an elegant formal basis for work in this area. Thus, the SECD machine evolved into an automaton that could be used to evaluate expressions of an applied λ-calculus. In this section, we discuss an algorithm that implements the SECD machine and some of the later extensions to the algorithm. In particular, we will extend the machine so that it supports the lazy evaluation of expressions. But first we present the notation that the machine implements.

Because the machine will have to be able to recognize the various types of expression, possibly access subcomponents of an expression and construct expressions from their subcomponents, instead of using BNF notation we will use structure definitions. A structure definition explicitly provides us with names for predicates and selectors, which provide a means of implementing the first two facilities, and also implicitly provides us with constructor names. The definition of an SECD machine expression is shown below:

```
An expression is
    an identifier
    or a λ-exp consisting of
                    a bvpart which is a variable name
                and a body which is an expression
    or an application consisting of
                    an operator which is an expression
                and an operand which is an expression
```

The predicates introduced in this definition are "expression", "identifier", "λ-exp" and "application". Selector names are defined as the names of subcomponents of a structure; thus "bvpart", "body", "operator" and "operand" are all selectors.

An identifier may be a variable name or any constant symbol within the notation; this includes the usual constants such as the integers and also the primitive functions, such as $+$ and $-$. It is clear from the definition of a λ-expression that our notation only allows one parameter functions, but this does not present a problem because we can always convert a multi-parameter function to an equivalent function that takes one parameter at a time. For example:

λ xy. x + y

becomes λ x.λ y. x + y

The example is not quite correct because the final clause of the structure definition requires that expressions be in prefix form, that is with the operator preceding its operand. Also, in future we shall omit all of the dots (.) except the one immediately preceding the body of the expression. Thus we should rewrite the function as follows:

λ x λ y. + x y

The final clause of the structure definition also provides us with the notation to represent non-recursive auxiliary definitions. We do this by adding parameters to the higher level definition which correspond to the auxiliary definitions. For example the SUGAR expression shown below would be translated as shown:

```
[ y ] { g ( y )
        where
        g is [ x ] x + 1
      }
```

becomes   (λ g λ y. g y) (λ x. + x 1)

We will discuss the implementation of conditionals, list constructs and recursive definitions after presenting the basic SECD machine.

The SECD machine uses four stacks in its operation which are called the Stack, the Environment, the Control and the Dump. At any time, the state of the machine is characterized by the values appearing on each of these stacks.

The Stack is used to store the partial results of evaluating an expression, and will hold the final result of the machine's execution.

The Environment consists of a series of pairs that give values to the free variables of an expression, the value of a constant in any environment being that constant. The first element of the pair is an identifier and the second element is the associated value.

The Control stores the expression that is being evaluated.

The Dump is used to store copies of the four stacks while a subfunction is being evaluated.

Since an SECD machine is intended to be an implementation of a functional language on a conventional, sequential machine, we use a conventional imperative design language to describe the operation. The top-level design of the machine is as follows:

```
WHILE there is an expression to be evaluated
      OR
      there is a suspended computation to be resumed
DO
    IF   the evaluation of the current expression is complete
    THEN resume the last suspended computation
         with the newly computed value on S
    ELSE
         CASE the next expression to be evaluated
            OF
              identifier:   push the value of this identifier
                                  onto S and pop C,
              λ-exp:        push the appropriate closure
                                  onto S and pop C,
              application: replace the top of C by the
                    expressions representing this application,
              "ap":         cause the operator on S to be applied
                                  to the operand below it
         ENDC;
    ENDF
ENDW
```

The closure referred to in the second case will have three components: the body of the λ-expression, the bound variable and an environment. Closures are equivalent to the funargs of Chapter 4, and ensure that the free variables are associated with the correct values when a function is evaluated. We will use the expressions "first(X)" for the top item on stack X and "rest(X)" for the stack which is left after first(X) has been popped. The phrases of the design may now be refined as follows:

```
there is an expression to be evaluated :-
    C is not empty
- - - - -
there is a suspended computation to be resumed :-
    D is not empty
- - - - -
the evaluation of the current expression is complete :-
    C is empty
- - - - -
resume the last suspended computation
        with the newly computed value on S :-
    remember the value on S;
    recover S,E,C,D from D;
    push the value from the old S onto S
- - - - -
the next expression to be evaluated :-
    top of C
- - - - -
push the value of this identifier onto S and pop C :-
    find the value of the identifier in E and push it onto S;
    pop C
- - - - -
push the appropriate closure onto S and pop C :-
    push the triple (body, bvpart, E) onto S;
    pop C
- - - - -
replace the top of C by the
        expressions representing this application :-
    pop C;
    push the "ap" operator onto C;
    push the operator to be applied onto C;
    push the operand onto C
- - - - -
cause the operator on S to be applied
        to the operand below it :-
    IF   the operator is a closure
    THEN produce the new set of stacks with which to
                                evaluate the closure
    ELSE #the operator is a primitive function #
        pop C;
        find the result of applying first(S) to
                                first(rest(S));
        pop S twice;
        push the result onto S
    ENDF
- - - - -
the operator is a closure :-
    first(S) is a closure
- - - - -
```

```
produce the new set of stacks with which to
        evaluate the closure :-
    push the quadruple ( rest(rest(S)), E, rest(C), D ) onto D;
    push the body of the closure onto a new empty C;
    make E the environment from the closure prefixed by a pair
    associating the bvpart of the closure with first(rest(S));
    create a new empty S
- - - - -
```

Now we show a walkthrough of $(\lambda x \lambda y.+xy)$ 3 4, with stacks growing to the right (i.e. stack top on the right) and commas separating stack elements:

```
S                          E              C                        D
                                          (λxλy.+xy) 3 4
                                          ap, (λxλy.+xy) 3, 4
4                                         ap, (λxλy.+xy) 3
4                                         ap, ap, (λxλy.+xy), 3
4,3                                       ap, ap, (λxλy.+xy)
4,3,cl(λy.+xy,x,())                       ap, ap
                           (x,3)          λy.+xy                   (4,(),ap,())
cl(+xy,y,(x,3))            (x,3)                                   (4,(),ap,())
4,cl(+xy,y,(x,3))                         ap
                           (x,3),(y,4)    + x y                    ((),(),(),())
                           (x,3),(y,4)    ap, + x, y               ((),(),(),())
4                          (x,3),(y,4)    ap, + x                  ((),(),(),())
4                          (x,3),(y,4)    ap, ap, +, x             ((),(),(),())
4,3                        (x,3),(y,4)    ap, ap, +                ((),(),(),())
4,3,+                      (x,3),(y,4)    ap, ap                   ((),(),(),())
4,+3                       (x,3),(y,4)    ap                       ((),(),(),())
7                          (x,3),(y,4)                             ((),(),(),())
7
```

A structure on the Stack that is prefixed by "cl" represents a closure. Note that this design enforces a call-by-value parameter passing mechanism; all parameters are evaluated before applications are evaluated. Shortly we shall see how the machine can be modified to support lazy evaluation. However, first we look at some simpler extensions that enable the machine to evaluate lists and support conditional and recursive computations, thus giving the power to implement the features of most functional languages.

To add lists to the SECD machine, we need a representation for the null list and constructor and selector functions. We shall write the null list as "<>". New lists may be constructed by adding items to the front using the prefix operator, ":" (which is added to our set of identifiers as a primitive function). We shall use an abbreviated notation that allows us to represent a series of items that are prefixed to the null list as a bracketed list.

```
1 : 2 : 3 : <> is equivalent to < 1, 2, 3 >
```

The set of identifiers is also augmented with two selector functions "h" and "t" (for head and tail). When a list is found on the Control all of its elements are evaluated as it is copied to the Stack (remember that the list notation is an abbreviation for a string of applications of the prefix operator). So for the application "h <1,2>" we get the following walkthrough:

```
S                E        C                              D

                          h <1,2>
                          ap, h, <1,2>
                          ap, h, ap, : 1, : 2 <>
                          ap, h, ap, : 1, ap, : 2, <>
<>                        ap, h, ap, : 1, ap, : 2
<>                        ap, h, ap, : 1, ap, ap, :, 2
<>, 2                     ap, h, ap, : 1, ap, ap, :
<>, 2, :                  ap, h, ap, : 1, ap, ap
<>, : 2                   ap, h, ap, : 1, ap
<2>                       ap, h, ap, : 1
<2>                       ap, h, ap, ap, :, 1
<2>, 1                    ap, h, ap, ap, :
<2>, 1, :                 ap, h, ap, ap
<2>, : 1                  ap, h, ap, ap
<1,2>                     ap, h, ap
<1,2>, h                  ap, h
1                         ap
```

Using the list notation we can define a conditional function in our set of primitive functions. The "if" function has two parameters, a boolean and a pair; it uses the boolean to select one element of the pair. Unfortunately there is a complication that prevents a simple-minded representation of conditionals as illustrated by the following example.

```
if (!= a 0) < / 1 a, a >
```

which is equivalent to

```
if a != 0 then 1 / a else a endf
```

If the above example appeared on the Control in an environment where "a" is defined to be zero, the SECD machine will execute an illegal divide-by-zero instruction. This is because both arms of the conditional are evaluated before the selection is made. This problem does not arise in the lazy version of the SECD machine that is presented at the end of this section. Within the call-by-value framework, the conventional solution, suggested by Burge and others, is to delay the evaluation of the conditional branches by introducing dummy parameters. The dummy parameter usually introduced is the empty list, <>, together with an empty list for the corresponding bound variable. If this solution is adopted, the conditional from the earlier example becomes:

```
( if ( != a 0 ) < λ<>./1a, λ<>.a > ) <>
```

In this way the two branches of the conditional become λ-expressions and their evaluation is thus delayed.

Finally, we look at the implementation of recursive functions. The usual approach is to include the Y function as one of the primitive functions (see Chapter 3 for a discussion of Y). Thus a factorial function would appear on the Control in the following form:

```
Y λf λn.( ( if (= n 0) < λ<>.1, λ<>.*nf(−n1) > ) ) <>
```

The problem of making successive copies of the function body available to the recursive calls is solved within the implementation of the primitive function Y.

An alternative approach might involve using the "labelling" notion introduced in the meta-circular interpreter. We would have to extend the structure definition by adding the following clause:

```
or a labelled exp consisting of a label which is an identifier
             and a lpart which is an expression
```

It would then be necessary to amend our program design in two places to allow for this new sort of expression. Firstly, an extra case in the top level design, to deal with such expressions on the control stack:

```
labelled exp: # augment the environment and begin
              execution #
              construct a pair of the label and
                     the lpart and push onto E;
              pop C;
              push the lpart from top of E onto C,
```

Secondly, to deal with the further possible operator that can appear on S waiting to be applied, the following code must be added to the refinement "cause the operator on S ... below it":

```
    ELSF the operator is a λ-exp
    THEN push the λ-exp onto C;
         pop S
```

It is left as an exercise for the reader to show how these alterations affect the execution of the machine.

We now look at how to extend the SECD machine to support lazy evaluation. In the lazy evaluation mechanism parameters for non-primitive functions are always passed in an unevaluated form. Primitive functions may be strict, such as $+$, requiring all of their parameters to be evaluated, or non-strict, such as lazy LISP-like "cons" and "&&" in SUGAR, that do not require all of their parameters to be evaluated. The SECD machine must remember enough information so that it can evaluate the parameters when they are required. It does this by means of a suspension which consists of an unevaluated parameter plus the environment in which it is to be evaluated. The complete development showing the required additions is shown below:

```
WHILE # there is an expression to be evaluated #
      C is not empty
    OR
    # there is a suspended computation to be resumed #
      D is not empty
DO
  IF   # the evaluation of the current expression is complete#
       C is empty
  THEN # resume the last suspended computation with the newly
                                       computed value on S #
    remember the value on S;
    recover S,E,C,D from D;
    push the value from the old S onto S
  ELSE
    CASE # the next expression to be evaluated #
         top of C
    OF
      "sp": # resume the last incomplete suspended computation
                 with all references to the completed suspension
                               replaced by the computed value #
           remember first(S);
           recover S,E,C and D from first(D);
           throughout S and E replace all occurrences of the
           suspension that is first(rest(S)) by what was first(S),
      identifier: # push the value of this identifier onto S and
                                                      pop C #
           find the value of this identifier in E and push it
                                                      onto S;
           pop C,
```

```
λ-exp: # push the appropriate closure onto S and pop C #
       push the triple (body, bvpart, E) onto S;
       pop C,
application: # replace the top of C by the expressions
                            representing this application #
       pop C;
       push the "ap" operator onto C;
       push the operator to be applied onto C;
       IF the operand is a function
       THEN push the operand onto C
       ELSE # create a suspension for the operator #
            push the pair ( operand, E ) onto S
       ENDF,
 "ap": # cause the operator on S to be applied to the operand
                                             below it #
       IF   # the operator is a closure #
            first(S) is a closure
       THEN # produce the new set of stacks with which to
                               evaluate the closure #
            push the quadruple
                    ( rest(rest(S)), E, rest(C), D) onto D;
            push the body of the closure onto a new empty C;
            make E the environment from the closure prefixed
                    by a pair associating the bvpart of the
                            closure with first(rest(S));
            create a new empty S
       ELSF # the operator is a strict primitive function and
                            its operand is a suspension #
            first(S) is strict
            AND first(rest(S)) is a suspension
       THEN # produce the new set of stacks with which to
                            evaluate the suspension #
            push the quadruple ( S, E, C, D ) onto D;
            push the "sp" operator onto C;
            push the body of the suspension onto C;
            push the environment of the suspension onto E;
            create a new empty S
       ELSE # the operator has its necessary operands #
            pop C;
            find the result of applying first(S) to
                                        first(rest(S));
            pop S twice;
            push the result onto S
       ENDF
    ENDC;
  ENDF
ENDW
```

We have introduced an "sp" operator on the Control that marks the
end of evaluation of a suspension. This is a different approach from
that proposed by Burge [Bu1] which involves an "assigning" Dump.

All non-functional parameters are copied from the Control to the Stack as suspensions; a suspension is represented as a structure preceded by "su" in the following examples. We illustrate the operation of the lazy SECD machine by two examples. The first example shows how the lazy machine avoids evaluating parameters that are not needed in the computation, whilst the conventional SECD machine evaluates all parameters and then throws the values away.

On the conventional machine:

```
S                        E                        C                    D
                         (y,6)                    (λx.4) y
                         (y,6)                    ap, (λx.4), y
6                        (y,6)                    ap, (λx.4)
6, cl(4,x,((y,6)))       (y,6)                    ap
                         (y,6), (x,6)             4                    D'
4                        (y,6), (x,6)                                  D'
4                        (y,6)
```

On the lazy machine:

```
S                        E                              C            D
                         (y,6)                          (λx.4) y
su(y,((y,6)))            (y,6)                          ap, (λx.4)
su(y,((y,6))),
   cl(4,x,((y,6)))       (y,6)                          ap
                         (y,6), (x,su(y,((y,6))))       4            D'
4                        (y,6), (x,su(y,((y,6))))                    D'
4                        (y,6)
```

where D' = ((), ((y,6)), (), ())

The importance of this feature is easier to see when considering examples such as an SECD version of the expression in Chapter 4.

(λx λy. + 3 y) ((λx. xx) (λx. xx)) 6

This would produce a non-terminating computation on the original SECD machine but the lazy machine terminates with the value 9 on the Stack as expected.

The second example shows a major benefit of lazy evaluation, which is that it allows us to deal with potentially infinite lists. For example, an infinite list of squares could be specified as follows:

In SUGAR

sq is [n] <n*n> && sq(n+1)

for the SECD machine

Y λsq. λn. (* n n) : (sq(+ n 1))

In the following example it is assumed that the environment E' binds an atomic value to "x" and that "y" is a possibly infinite list (which of course would have to be stored in a "suspended" form).

S	E	C	D
	E'	h(: x y)	
su(: x y,E')	E'	ap, h	
su(: x y,E'), h	E'	ap	
	E'	sp, : x y	D'
su(y,E')	E'	sp, ap, : x	D'
su(y,E'), su(x,E')	E'	sp, ap, ap, :	D'
su(y,E'), su(x,E'), :	E'	sp, ap, ap	D'
su(y,E'), : su(x,E')	E'	sp, ap	D'
<su(x,E'), su(y,E')>	E'	sp	D'
<su(x,E'), su(y,E')>, h	E'	ap	
su(x,E')	E'		

where D' = ((su(: x y,E'),h), E', ap, ())

The machine terminates with a suspension on the top of the stack. A complete implementation of the lazy SECD machine would include a strict print function that could be used as the last step to evaluate the suspension. The walkthrough shown above contrasts with the conventional machine that would have also evaluated the whole of y and then thrown it away.

This completes our discussion of the SECD machine and we now turn our attention to a more recent implementation technique based on the use of combinators.

EXERCISES

1. Show a walkthrough for the following expression on the conventional SECD machine:

(λfλxλy . +(fx)(fy)) square 3 4

where "square" is the primitive squaring function.

2. Repeat Exercise 1 for the lazy SECD machine.

3. Show a walkthrough for the following expression on the lazy SECD machine:

$(\lambda x\ \lambda y.\ +\ 3\ y\ )\ (\ (\lambda x.\ xx)\ (\lambda x.\ xx)\ )\ 6$

4. Modify the lazy SECD machine to support call-by-name parameter passing.

5. Implement the lazy SECD machine in a suitable programming language.

6. Rewrite the "sq" function using a labelled expression and show a walkthrough on the lazy SECD machine for:

```
h( t( "your SECD sq function"(2)))
```

5.2 THE SK-REDUCTION MACHINE

The machine that we are going to describe in this section executes a program that is represented as a graph of combinators and constant identifiers. Combinators were first introduced by Schönfinkel in the early twenties and they grew out of the same area of logic that later produced the λ-calculus. Schönfinkel showed how, by using a small set of combinators, it is possible to remove all variables from a functional expression producing a new expression that merely consists of some combinators and other constant symbols (such as the integers and primitive function symbols). Later on we shall define this translation process but first we define some useful combinators in λ-calculus terms and discuss the implications of using combinators to implement functional languages.

A selection of the combinators are shown below.

name	combinator	λ-calculus definition
identity	I	$\lambda x.\ x$
permutator	C	$\lambda fxy.\ f\ y\ x$
compositor	B	$\lambda fxy.\ f\ (\ x\ y\ )$
cancellator	K	$\lambda xy.\ x$
distributor	S	$\lambda xyz.\ x\ z\ (\ y\ z\ )$
fixed point combinator	Y	$\lambda h.\ ((\ \lambda x.\ h(xx)\ )(\ \lambda x.\ h(xx)))$

We introduced S, K, I, B and Y in Chapter 3 and showed that I was convertible with SKK. In fact there is a theoretical result that shows that all of the other combinators can be defined in terms of S and K, so in that sense there are only two "primitive" combinators. The SK-reduction machine uses all of the combinators shown above and a few other specialized combinators which we shall not mention further. The major advantage that accrues from using "combinator code" as a machine code is that, as there are no variables, there is no need to maintain an environment. The SK-reduction machine provides the same facilities as the lazy SECD machine in that non-strict functions are supported and expressions are only evaluated once.

Before looking at the SK-reduction machine, we turn our attention to the compilation process that converts a functional expression into combinator code. We illustrate the process using the notation defined by the structure definitions of the last section, which are repeated below.

```
An expression is
      an identifier
      or a λ-exp consisting of
                      a bvpart which is a variable name
                      and a body which is an expression
      or an application consisting of
                      an operator which is an expression
                      and an operand which is an expression
```

Initially we suppose that the compiler will generate code using only the S, K and I combinators. We then go on to consider how optimized code may be produced, since we will find that the code produced by this first version can be very complicated even for quite trivial functions. The combinators B and C will be introduced as part of the code improvement process; the combinator Y is only used in the translation of auxiliary definitions, described later.

The compilation of identifiers and applications is a straightforward process. Free-standing identifiers are left as they are while the operator and operand of an application are compiled separately and the compiled operator is juxtaposed with the compiled operand. The compilation of a λ-exp is slightly more complicated because we must consider the structure of the body of the expression before deciding what to produce.

When the body is an identifier we get two subcases; the first deals with the situation that the body is equal to the bound variable of the λ-exp, the second deals with all other cases. Below we show what the compile function "cmp" would produce when applied to the λ-exp, E.

```
when E is the λ-exp λx.x then I
                # since λx.x is I #
when E is the λ-exp λx.y then K y
                # since λx.y cnv ( λzx. z ) y
                and λzx.z cnv K #
```

When the body is itself a λ-exp, we compile the body before compiling the whole expression. This is defined as shown below.

```
when E is the λ-exp λx.λy.E' then cmp( λx. cmp( λy.E'))
```

Finally, when the body is an application, F A say, the body is transformed as follows before compilation.

```
λx. F A        cnv     λx. ( λx. F ) x (( λx. A ) x )
```

The right hand expression explicitly shows the bound variable of the original expression being distributed to the two subcomponents of the application. The compilation of a λ-exp whose body is an application is now shown below.

```
when E is the λ-exp λx.F A then S ( cmp( λx. F )) ( cmp(λx. A))
        # since λx. ( λx. F ) x ( ( λx. A ) x )
        cnv ( λfax. fx ( ax ) ) ( λx. F ) ( λx. A )
        which is S ( λx. F ) ( λx. A )
        and cmp ( S ( λx. F ) ( λx. A ))
        ==> cmp ( S ( λx. F ) ) ( cmp ( λx. A ) )
        ==> cmp ( S ) ( cmp ( λx. F )) ( cmp ( λx. A ))
        ==> S ( cmp ( λx. F )) ( cmp ( λx. A ))
        #
```

That deals with all of the possibilities for the body of the λ-exp. We can now present a complete definition of the function.

```
cmp ( E ) is
     when E is an identifier then E
     when E is the λ-exp λx.x then I
     when E is the λ-exp λx.y then K y
     when E is the λ-exp λx.λy.E' then cmp( λx. cmp( λy.E'))
     when E is the λ-exp λx.F A then S(cmp(λx.F)) (cmp(λx.A))
     when E is the application F A then cmp(F) cmp(A)
     otherwise  error in expression
```

We conclude this initial treatment of the translation process by looking at two examples. At each stage the applications of "cmp" that have been selected for evaluation are underlined. The first example is an expression that represents the successor function.

cmp (λx. + x 1)

    ==> S cmp (λx. + x) cmp (λx.1)

    ==> S (S cmp (λx.+) cmp (λx.x)) cmp (λx.1)

    ==> S (S (K +) I) (K 1)

The second, more complicated, example involves the abstraction of two variables from an expression. We illustrate this by a function that adds its two parameters.

cmp(λx λy. + x y)

==> cmp(λx. S cmp(λy.+ x) cmp(λy.y))

==> cmp(λx. S (S cmp(λy.+) cmp(λy.x)) cmp(λy.y))

==> cmp(λx. S (S (K +) (K x)) I)

==> S cmp(λx. S (S (K +) (K x))) cmp(λx.I)

==> S (S cmp(λx.S) cmp(λx.S (K +) (K x))) (K I)

==> S (S (K S) (S cmp(λx.S (K +)) cmp(λx.K x))) (K I)

==> S (S (KS)(S (S cmp(λx.S) cmp(λx.K +))
                  (S cmp(λx.K) cmp(λx.x)))) (K I)

==> S (S (K S) (S (S (K S) (S cmp(λx.K) cmp(λx.+)))
                     (S (K K) I))) (K I)

==> S (S (K S) (S (S (K S) (S (K K) (K +))) (S (K K) I))) (K I)

This function is, of course, only another definition of the primitive operator plus, but it shows clearly that the translation process as described above can yield long strings of combinator code for very simple expressions. Fortunately it is possible to optimize this code; the most important of the optimizations performed by David Turner's compiler are motivated by the following equivalences:

```
1. S (K E1) (K E2)    =      (λxyz. xz(yz)) (K E1) (K E2)
                      cnv    λz. K E1 z ( K E2 z )
                      =      λz. (λxy. x) E1 z ( (λxy. x) E2 z )
                      cnv    λz. E1 E2
                      cnv    ( λxz. x ) ( E1 E2 )
                      =      K ( E1 E2 )

2. S (K E1) I         =      λz. K E1 z ( I z )
                      cnv    λz. E1 z
                      cnv    E1

3. S (K E1) E2        =      λz. K E1 z ( E2 z )
                      cnv    λz. E1 ( E2 z )
                      cnv    ( λfgz. f ( g z )) E1 E2
                      =      B E1 E2

4. S E1 (K E2)        =      λz. E1 z (K E2 z)
                      cnv    λz. E1 z E2
                      cnv    ( λfgz. f z g ) E1 E2
                      =      C E1 E2
```

Optimizations 3 and 4 are only used if optimizations 1 and 2 are not applicable.

These optimizations could be performed on the code produced by "cmp", but it will be very much more efficient if the optimizations are performed during the translation process, for then the substrings of code which have to be handled by outer levels of the recursion are smaller at each stage. Thus we modify the definition of "cmp", at the point where it produces code of the form S E1 E2, checking to see if in fact simpler code could be generated because one of the optimizations 1 to 4 is applicable. We now have:

```
cmp ( E ) is
         when E is an identifier then E
         when E is the λ-exp λx.x then I
         when E is the λ-exp λx.y then K y
         when E is the λ-exp λx.λy.E' then cmp( λx. cmp( λy.E'))
         when E is the λ-exp λx.F A then
                 opt( cmp( λx.F ), cmp( λx.A ) )
         when E is the application F A then cmp(F) cmp(A)
         otherwise  error in expression
```

where opt is defined as follows:

```
opt( E1, E2 ) is
        when E1 is of the form K E3 and
             E2 of the form K E4 then K(E3 E4)
        when E1 is of the form K E3 and E2 is I then E3
        when E1 is of the form K E3 then B E3 E2
        when E2 is of the form K E4 then C E1 E4
        otherwise S E1 E2
```

The successor function shown earlier is now translated as follows:

```
cmp( λx. + x 1)
    ==> opt( cmp( λx. + x ), cmp( λx. 1 ) )
    ==> opt( opt( cmp( λx. + ), cmp( λx. x ) ), K 1)
    ==> opt( opt( K +, I ), K 1)
    ==> opt( +, K 1 )
    ==> C + 1
```

For the addition function, the translation is as follows:

```
cmp( λx.λy. + x y )
    ==> cmp( λx. cmp( λy. + x y ) )
    ==> cmp( λx. opt( cmp( λy. + x ), cmp( λy.y ) ) )
    ==> cmp( λx. opt( opt( cmp( λy.+ ), cmp( λy.x ) ), I ) )
    ==> cmp( λx. opt( opt( K +, K x), I ) )
    ==> cmp( λx. opt( K( + x ), I ) )
    ==> cmp( λx. + x )
    ==> cmp( opt( cmp( λx.+ ), cmp( λx.x )) )
    ==> cmp( opt( K +, I ) )
    ==> cmp( + )
    ==> +
```

Using this optimizing version of "cmp" it is now quite possible to compile non-trivial functions by hand. Before giving an example, we point out the following property of this new version:

```
when E does not contain any free occurrences of x,
    cmp(λx.E) = K E
```

This property will prove to be useful in the following example:

```
cmp(λx.λy. sqrt(+ (* x x) (* y y)))
==> cmp(λx. cmp(λy. sqrt(+ (* x x)(* y y))))
==> cmp(λx.opt(cmp(λy. sqrt), cmp(λy. +(* x x)(* y y))))
==> cmp(λx.opt(K sqrt, opt(cmp(λy +(* x x)), cmp(λy.* y y))))
==> cmp(λx.opt(K sqrt,opt(K(+(* x x)),opt(cmp(λy.* y),cmp(λy.y)))))
==> cmp(λx.opt(K sqrt, opt(K(+(* x x)), opt(*, I))))
==> cmp(λx.opt(K sqrt, opt(K(+(*x x)), (S*I))))
```

```
==> cmp(λx.opt(K sqrt, B (+(* x x)) (S*I)))
==> cmp(λx.B sqrt (B(+(*x x))(S*I)))
==> opt(cmp(λx.B sqrt), cmp(λx. B(+(* x x))S*I))
==> opt(K(B sqrt), opt(cmp(λx.B(+(*x x))), cmp(λx.S*I)))
==> opt(K(B sqrt), opt(opt(cmp(λx.B), cmp(λx.+(*x x))),K(S*I)))
==> opt(K(B sqrt), opt(opt(KB,opt(cmp(λx.+),cmp(λx.*x x))),K(S*I)))
==> opt(K(B sqrt), opt(opt(KB, opt(K+, S*I)), K(S*I)))
==> opt(K(B sqrt), opt(opt(KB, B+(S*I)), K(S*I)))
==> opt(K(B sqrt), opt(BB(B+(S*I)), K(S*I)))
==> opt(K(B sqrt), C(BB(B+(S*I)))(S*I))
==> B(B sqrt)(C(BB(B+(S*I)))(S*I))
```

Having looked at the compilation process which produces combinator code for the SK-reduction machine, we now return to considering the machine itself. Instead of using the "if" function defined in the last section, the SK-reduction machine has a primitive "cond" function that takes three parameters: a boolean and expressions for each of the two branches of the conditional.

As stated earlier, the combinator code is stored in graphical form. Recursion in the top-level expression is represented by a cyclic pointer in the graph, Y is only used for recursive auxiliary definitions. The representation of recursion by cyclic graphs is illustrated later in this section when we discuss the SK-reduction mechanism. Below, for comparison, we illustrate how the code for a simple recursive function is represented on the SECD machine (lazy version) and the SK-reduction machine.

SECD:
```
        Y λf λn. if (= 1 n) < 1, + n ( f ( − n 1 ) ) >
```

SK (source code):
```
        sum = λn. cond (= 1 n) 1 (+ n ( sum ( − n 1 ) ) )
```

SK (combinator code):
```
        sum = S(C(B cond ( = 1 )) 1)(S + (B sum ( C − 1 )))
```

Auxiliary definitions are handled in the same way as they were in the SECD machine. A bound variable is added to the top-level definition and the expression on the right hand side of the auxiliary definition is passed as a parameter. Thus, for example, the following transformation is performed before the combinator code is produced:

$\lambda x. \ g \ x \ 2$
$\qquad$ where
$\qquad\qquad g = \lambda z \ \lambda y. \ \text{**} \ z \ y$
becomes
$\qquad (\lambda g. \ (\lambda x. \ g \ x \ 2) \ ) \ (\lambda z. \ (\lambda y. \ \text{**} \ z \ y \ ))$

If the auxiliary definitions involve recursion they are compiled to code which uses the Y combinator as intimated earlier. Therefore, if the "sum" function is defined in an auxiliary definition, it is transformed to a form that is equivalent to the SECD code before translation to pure combinator code.

We now turn our attention to the SK-reduction machine.

We have already indicated that the combinator code is stored as a graph in the SK-reduction machine. In fact this graph has binary nodes containing either combinators, basic identifiers (the primitive functions, truth values, integers, etc.) or pointers to other nodes. The structure of the graph mirrors the applicative structure of the original code. For example, the "sum" code is illustrated below.

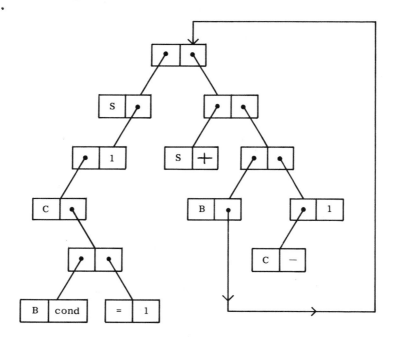

A function application is represented by a node whose left subgraph is the function graph and whose right subgraph is the operand value. Given the equivalences between the combinators and λ-calculus expressions it should be clear what is meant when we refer to a redex in a combinator string (see Chapter 3). The SK-reduction machine "collapses" the graph of combinators by reducing redexes and by replacing the parent node of the redex either by pointers to the reduced expression or by a primitive value. The process that we have described above is called graph reduction. In fact the SK-reduction machine carries out normal graph reduction in that the leftmost redex is always reduced first. This leftmost redex may be found by starting at the root of the graph and moving to the left until a reducible operator is found. When a primitive operator whose operand is not a primitive value is encountered, the search proceeds down the operand branch.

The reduction rules that the SK-reduction machine uses can be inferred from the λ-calculus definitions of the combinators. The rules for S, K, I, B and C are shown below:

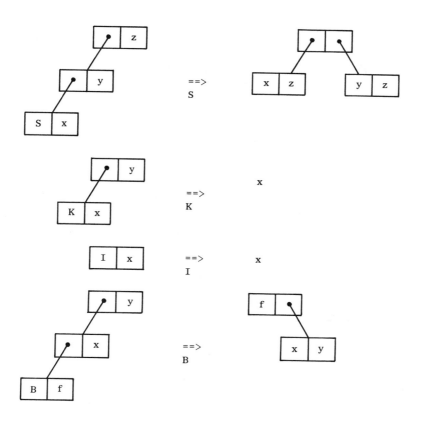

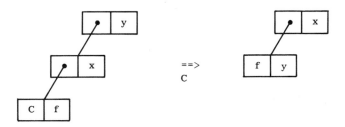

The reduction rules for K and I cause the graph to be reduced to a single value which may be a pointer to a subgraph or a literal value. The rule for Y is slightly less straightforward than the others since the λ-calculus definition would imply an infinite graph. Instead the infinite graph is represented by a finite cyclic graph and the reduction rule is shown below.

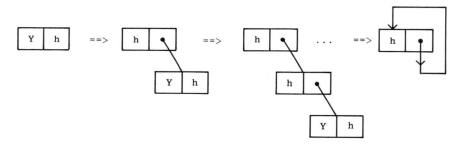

The reduction process terminates either when there are no further redexes (in which case the expression was not evaluable), or when the graph has been reduced to a single node which is a "printable" object. We illustrate the reduction process for an application of the optimized successor function to the value 2.

Finally, in order to illustrate the graph reductions for S, K and I we illustrate the reduction process for the unoptimized version of the successor function applied to 2. For ease of reference the leftmost redex at each stage has been marked with an asterisk.

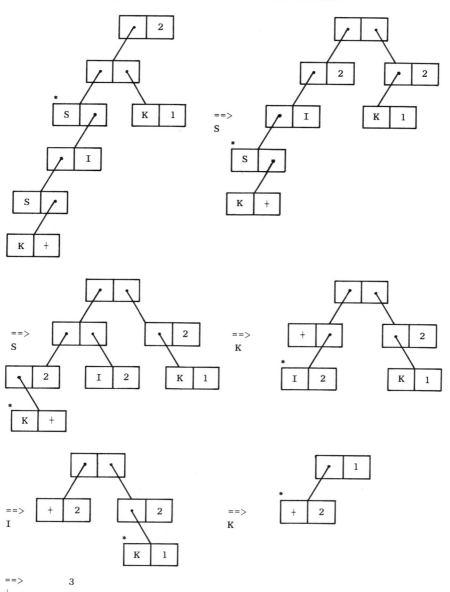

EXERCISES

1. Compute optimized combinator code for the function $\lambda fx.\ fxx$. (This function is the W combinator.)

2. Compute optimized combinator code for the function

   λn. cond (<= 1 n) 1 (+ n (sum (− n 1)))

mentioned earlier in this section.

3. For the optimizing version of "cmp" show that

   cmp(λx.E) = K E if and only if x is not free in E.

4. Suggest how W may be used in an optimization rule for SK-machine code, giving a modified definition of "opt" which takes account of this rule.

5. Derive optimized combinator code for Y, using this modified "opt".

6. Draw the SK-reduction machine graph of the code produced from Exercise 1 and show the reduction sequence when the function is applied with times and 2 as the parameters.

5.3 DATA FLOW MACHINES

In this last section, we look at the way in which functional programs may be translated so that they run on data flow machines. This section looks to the future in that, at the time of writing, only prototype data flow machines have been produced and none of these easily supports higher order functions. Hence the data flow notation that we use does not conform to the machine code of any of the prototypes but is instead oriented towards the flexible support of higher order functions.

The name "data flow" has been coined to refer to systems which instead of having a centralized control unit and program counter, select operations for execution when their operands have been computed. In this sense, the flow of data between operations provides the sequencing control that is normally provided by the program counter in a conventional "control flow" machine. Because the operands of several operators may be available simultaneously, the data flow approach also facilitates the exploitation of parallelism in a program. Data flow systems are relevant because they share the property of referential transparency with functional systems, since they do not have the concept of global memory.

Data flow programs are usually represented as directed graphs where the nodes represent operators and the arcs show the data dependencies between operators. We constrain the graph to be acyclic; this is not a universal constraint but it does simplify the properties of the graph and closely mirrors the approach taken in the other two systems described in this chapter. In the following diagrams, the data flow is always directed down the page. The notation consists of a set of five basic operator types, a function application operator and a notation for function definition. Inputs and outputs to and from a graph are shown as arcs that are only connected to the graph at one end. The basic operators are shown below.

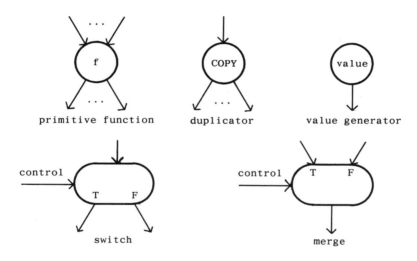

All data dependencies are explicitly shown in the graph, so that if two operators use the same value, they must both have an input arc that emanates from the same place. There is an explicit duplicate node that may be used to provide the appropriate number of copies of a value. The value generator is the operator used to insert literal values onto the graph at run-time; literal values include the integers, booleans and other primitive types as well as function identifiers (see below). The switch and merge operators are used to construct conditional computations. For example, the cond function of the SK-reduction machine might appear as shown below:

"cond P A B" becomes

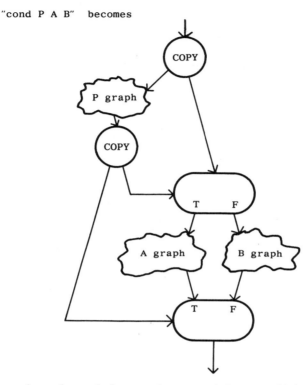

At run-time the switch uses its control input, which is a boolean, to select one of its output arcs to receive the input value. Similarly, the merge uses its control input to select a value from one of its input arcs. The above graph assumes that both A and B are only dependent on one value. If this were not the case the conditional graph would require multiple switches and merges, one pair for each value, all taking their control input from the P graph.

A graph may be defined as a function by enclosing it in a "box". The arcs entering the box represent the bound variables of the function and the arc emanating from the box represents the result of the function. The name of the function is written in the bottom left hand corner of the box. All user-defined functions are assumed to be curried. An application of a user-defined function is represented by an explicit apply node. The apply node takes two inputs, a function name or closure and a parameter value. Function names may be written explicitly at the node or may be passed on an input arc as are function closures. The apply node produces a value or a function closure as its result depending on whether the applied function was a first order function (or a function closure whose body is a first order function) or a higher order function. The apply node is conceptually replaced by a copy of the function body when a first order function or closure body is applied. The apply node is shown below.

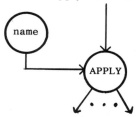

Recursive function definitions are represented by boxed graphs containing self-referential apply nodes. For example, the data flow graph for the SUGAR factorial function:

```
fac is [n] if n = 0 then 1
           else n * fac(n-1)
           endf ;
```

is shown in Figure 5.1.

When the parameter is zero the computation of the result is independent of the parameter and thus the T output of the switch is not required. This is indicated by omitting the T output arc from the switch.

There are two approaches to the evaluation of data flow programs; one is the classical data-driven approach which is a call-by-value mechanism and the other is the demand-driven approach which provides lazy evaluation. Following the approach used earlier in this section we will describe each mechanism at an abstract level within the context of the data flow notation that we have presented.

First, we define a data-driven mechanism. We need a representation for data flow instructions, and a structure definition of the representation that we shall use is shown below:

```
A data flow instruction consists of
        an input record which has a field for each input
        an identifier
        a type which is one of the basic operators or apply
        an output list which is a list of instruction identifier/
                input field name pairs
```

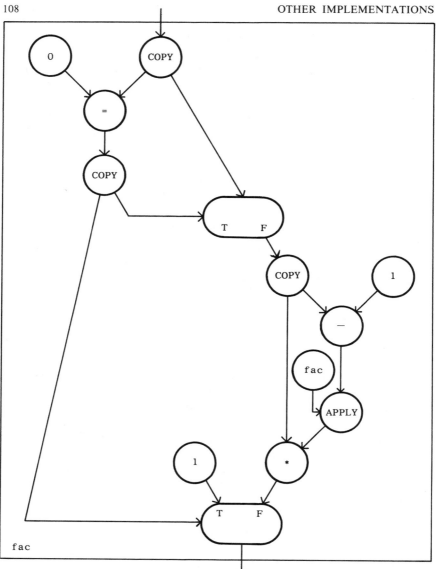

Figure 5.1

Each value produced from the execution of an instruction must be directed to a particular input arc of some instruction. Therefore we need a way of uniquely identifying instructions and a way of distinguishing between input arcs. We have used a record with named fields to represent the set of input arcs and each instruction has a unique identifier. Destinations for each of the results of an instruction are specified in the output list which contains one instruction/input field pair for each output arc. The type of the instruction identifies which operation is to be performed, which in the case of value generators and primitive functions must include information about which specific instance of the class is required. An example of a data flow program in this notation is shown below:

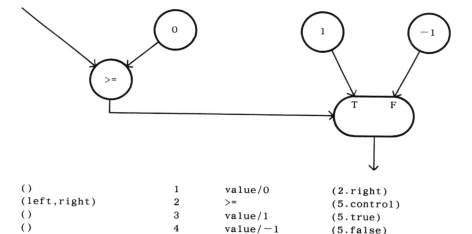

```
()                          1    value/0      (2.right)
(left,right)                2    >=           (5.control)
()                          3    value/1      (5.true)
()                          4    value/-1     (5.false)
(control,true,false)        5    merge        (*)
```

This is a program that returns the sign of its input, which arrives in the "left" input field of instruction 2. As we noted earlier, outputs emanate from a particular instruction but are not directed towards any instruction. This is represented in the code by an asterisk in the output list of an instruction.

The major cycle of the execution mechanism is shown below. There may be several different instances of this cycle active at any one time and each operates asynchronously with the others:

```
FOR any instruction DO
        IF the instruction has all of its required inputs
        THEN execute the instruction
        ENDF
ENDD
```

The refinements for the two main phrases are shown below:

```
the instruction has all of its required inputs :-
CASE type of instruction OF
    value : true,
    primitive, copy, switch, apply :
            IF all fields in the input record contain values
            THEN true
            ELSE false
            ENDF,
    merge : IF the control input field and the appropriate other
                            input field contain values
            THEN true
            ELSE false
            ENDF
ENDC
- - - - -
execute the instruction :-
CASE type of instruction OF
    primitive : perform the operation using the inputs;
                FOR each instruction in the output list DO
                    put the appropriate result in the specified
                    input field
                ENDD,
    copy : FOR each instruction in the output list DO
                put the value from the input record into the
                specified input field
            ENDD,
    value : put the value into the specified input field;
    switch : IF the control input is TRUE
             THEN place the other input value in the
                  specified input field of the first instruction
                  in the output list
             ELSE place the other input value in the
                  specified input field of the second instruction
                  in the output list
             ENDF,
    merge : IF the control input is TRUE
            THEN place the second (true) input value in the
                 input field specified in the output list
            ELSE place the third (false) input value in the
                 input field specified in the output list
            ENDF,
    apply : IF the first input is a single parameter function
            THEN generate a copy of the function;
                 place the second input value in the input record
                 of the first instruction in the function
            ELSE IF the first input is a closure which requires
                    a single parameter
                 THEN generate a copy of the function;
                      pass the second input and the closure values
```

```
                              to the input records of the appropriate
                              instructions;
                    ELSE generate a new closure with the second input
                              value
                    ENDF
              ENDF
ENDC;
delete the instruction;
```

A value operation always has its required inputs; all other operations require a complete set of inputs, except merge which only requires its control input and the selected input. With the exception of apply, the execution mechanism is straightforward. In the case of apply it is necessary to distinguish between an application that is providing the last parameter to a function or closure, in which case a copy of the function is generated ready for execution, and the other cases where a new closure is produced. The new copy of a function has to be "knitted into" the program by setting up the input records of initial instructions with parameter values and ensuring that the function output instructions send their results to the correct destinations. The generation process is refined below:

```
generate a copy of the function :-
create a new copy of each instruction in the function,
        assigning unique identifiers and changing the output
        lists accordingly;
FOR each output instruction in the function DO
        set the output list to the appropriate values from the
              output list of the apply operator
ENDD;
```

Since the program is acyclic and instructions are thus only executed once, each instruction is deleted after it has been executed.

As an example of this process we show how the sign program would be executed when the input is 5. Each snapshot in the trace results from executing all possible instructions:

```
Step 1:
    ()                                 1    value/0      (2.right)
    (left:5,right)                     2    >=           (5.control)
    ()                                 3    value/1      (5.true)
    ()                                 4    value/-1     (5.false)
    (control,true,false)              5    merge        (*)

Step 2:
    (left:5,right:0)                   2    >=           (5.control)
    (control,true:1,false:-1)          5    merge        (*)
```

```
Step 3:
  (control:TRUE,true:1,false:-1)   5     merge              (*)

Step 4:
  1
```

In demand-driven systems the computation is controlled by a combination of the presence of operands and a request for the result of an operation. Effectively, a structure is imposed on the program which carries requests in the reverse direction to the flow of data. This requirement is reflected in an extended definition of a data flow instruction:

```
A data flow instruction consists of
      a source list which is a list of instruction identifiers
      an input record which has a field for each input
      an identifier
      a type which is one of the basic operators or apply
      an output list which is a list of instruction identifier/
            input field name pairs
```

The main execution cycle is also more complicated. Only instructions whose results have been requested are executed and then only if the required operands have been computed, otherwise the request is propagated. The mechanism is defined below:

```
FOR any instruction whose output has been requested DO
    IF the instruction has all of its required inputs
    THEN execute the instruction
    ELSE CASE type of instruction OF
            primitive,copy,switch :
                    send the request to all instructions
                    in the source list,
            merge : IF control input is present
                    THEN IF control value is true
                            THEN send the request to the second
                                instruction in the source list
                            ELSE send the request to the third
                                instruction in the source list
                            ENDF
                    ELSE send request to first instruction
                            in the source list
                    ENDF,
            apply : send the request to the first instruction
                    in the source list
            ENDC
        ENDF
    ENDD
```

Requests are only propagated on input arcs that do not already contain values and thus "send the request" must take account of this. (A value may already be present as the result of the execution of a copy which was requested at its other output arc.) Only the inputs that are needed by merge are requested. The control input is requested first and then either the true input or the false input is requested, depending on the control value. The refinements for "the instruction has all of its required inputs" and "execute the instruction" are the same as the data-driven version except for the apply operator. The apply operator only requires its left input, the function or closure name, and is executed in the following way:

```
apply : IF the first input is a single parameter function
        THEN generate a new copy of the function
        ELSE IF the first input is a closure which requires
                a single parameter
             THEN generate a new copy of the function
             ELSE generate a new closure remembering the identifier
                  of the second instruction in the source list
             ENDF
        ENDF
```

In this mechanism, a closure consists of the function name and a list of instruction identifiers that are the sources of its parameters. The parameters may thus be requested, if required, when the function is evaluated. The generation of a function copy is refined below:

```
generate a new copy of the function :-
create a new copy of each instruction in the function, assigning
        unique identifiers and changing the source and output
        lists accordingly;
FOR each input instruction in the function DO
        set up the source list
ENDD;
FOR each output instruction in the function DO
        set the output list to the appropriate values from the
                output list of the apply operator;
        request the output if required
ENDD
```

This mechanism provides lazy evaluation (assuming a lazy constructor for lists) because values are only computed when they are required and once a value has been computed it will be available to any later requests. (This is because copy sends its result to all instructions in its output list, even if they have not all requested the value.)

We will not attempt to describe a data flow computer in this section, because so much work is still required in this area. A generalized block diagram of a data flow processor is shown below.

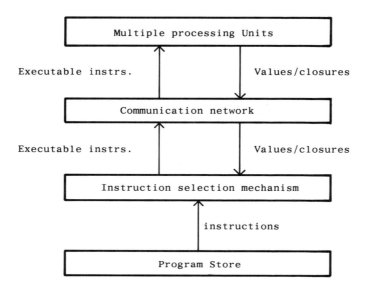

The various architectures that have been proposed are characterized by the different designs of the communications network. The two most popular approaches are to have a tree-structured network and to use multiple rings with a small number of processors on each ring. The demand-driven system designed at Utah is of the former variety and the data-driven machine built at Manchester University is of the latter variety.

That concludes our brief overview of the work that has been done on data flow systems. The interested reader is referred to Treleaven et al. [Tre] for a more detailed overview of actual systems.

EXERCISES

1. Convert a selection of SUGAR programs to data flow graphs.

2. Give a trace of the execution of the "sign" program by the demand-driven mechanism.
(Hint : There are two phases to this — the propagation of requests and then the arrival of data. However, they are intermingled.)

3. Trace the execution of an application of factorial to 2 using both of the execution mechanisms.

BIBLIOGRAPHY

Henderson describes the mechanism of the SECD machine in great detail, showing how the machine might be implemented. Higher level overviews of the operation of the SECD machine can be found in Burge and in Wegner. The description of the lazy SECD machine in this chapter is based on Burge's exposition of the subject.

Details of combinator-based implementation of functional languages may be found in Burge and in Turner. A formal treatment of combinatory logic is provided by Curry and Feys, although this is not recommended for the faint-hearted.

There has been little published in book form about data flow systems. Most of the literature takes the form of research papers. A recent survey of the area is to be found in Treleaven et al.

[Bu1] Burge W.H. "Recursive Programming Techniques", Addison-Wesley, 1975.

[Cur] Curry H.B. and Feys R. "Combinatory Logic, Volume 1", North-Holland, 1968.

[Hen] Henderson P. "Functional Programming: Application and Implementation", Prentice-Hall International, 1980.

[Tre] Treleaven P.C., Brownbridge D.R. and Hopkins R.P. "Data-Driven and Demand-Driven Computer Architecture", ACM Computing Surveys, Vol.14, No.1, March 1982.

[Tur] Turner D.A. "A New Implementation Technique for Applicative Languages", Software Practice and Experience, Vol.9, January 1979.

[Weg] Wegner P. "Programming Languages, Information Structures and Machine Organisation", McGraw-Hill, 1971.

6

FORMAL SEMANTICS

We have suggested that one of the advantages of using a functional language is that it is relatively easy to prove properties of programs. In order to do this we require formal definitions of all aspects of the language. Backus Naur Form has provided us with a way of formalizing the syntax of a language and in this chapter we will describe a notation that may be used to formalize the semantics. A formal semantics provides us with three things. Firstly, a yardstick with which to compare different implementations of a language; secondly, a framework for formal proofs of the correctness of individual programs; and thirdly, the basis of a method for automatically generating implementations.

There are several alternative approaches to the definition of the formal semantics of a language. The three established alternatives are Axiomatic Semantics, Operational Semantics and Denotational Semantics. The axiomatic approach involves defining the state change that takes place when each type of construct is executed. This framework provides an elegant basis for program correctness proofs in imperative languages but not for functional programming languages because it is involved with the concept of state change. An operational semantics specifies a language by defining an interpreter for the abstract syntax of the language. In a sense Chapter 5 was concerned with possible operational semantics of functional programming languages. The approach clearly gives pointers to methods that may be used in implementing a language; however, program proving is an unwieldy process which involves "cranking the handle" and showing a complete machine execution of the program. We have chosen to use denotational semantics because, although the other two approaches have their strong points, we feel that it is the only approach that is applicable in all of the areas that we have said that formal descriptions are useful.

The denotational semantics of a language defines what each grammatical unit denotes in some well-defined mathematical model. The meaning of a particular syntactic construct is defined in terms of the meanings of its immediate subcomponents. The Backus Naur Form that we have used elsewhere in this book specifies "concrete" syntax. Each clause defines how a particular construct looks when it is written down (or typed in) and thus contains lexical details that are inessential to the semantics of the language. A denotational description of a language employs an abstract syntax that specifies just enough about the syntax of the language to allow us to specify the semantics in an unambiguous fashion. The approach was originally devised by Christopher Strachey at Oxford University in the mid-sixties. It posed several seemingly paradoxical mathematical problems which were solved by Dana Scott, who joined Strachey at Oxford. Their approach can be understood without a deep understanding of the underlying mathematics and thus we postpone a treatment of this until Section 6.3. First we introduce a simple example of the notation, illustrating how the semantics may be used in correctness proofs, and then we present the denotational semantics of SUGAR.

The denotational description of an imperative programming language can become extremely complicated, but most of the complication arises from the handling of continuations, a concept introduced to handle jumps, and other complex features that are not required for functional programming languages. We do not cover these topics in this chapter and the reader is referred to the bibliography for more details.

6.1 AN INTRODUCTORY EXAMPLE

A denotational description of a language consists of five subcomponents:

```
a) Syntactic Domains
b) Abstract Syntax
c) Semantic Domains
d) Semantic Functions
e) Semantic Equations
```

Components a, b and d are to do with the naming and typing of objects, while b and e contain the main aspects of the definition. A "domain" is a restricted form of set, so that while all domains are sets, not all sets are domains. The denotational semantics effectively describes a series of mappings from elements of the syntactic domains to elements of the semantic domains.

A Syntactic Domain is the set of well-formed constructs generated by the corresponding clause of the abstract syntax.

The Abstract Syntax defines the format of elements of each of the syntactic domains.

A Semantic Domain is the set of values which denote the elements of some syntactic domain(s).

The Semantic Functions define the "type", a pairing of syntactic domains with semantic domains, of each function used to define the mappings of the definition.

The Semantic Equations define each mapping by its effect on elements of the appropriate syntactic domain.

We illustrate how each of the sections is defined by reference to a simple example, the semantics of binary numerals. First of all, we clarify the difference between numerals and numbers. A numeral is a collection of graphic symbols that represents a number. The same number may be represented by different numerals; a familiar example being the use of Arabic and Roman numerals. In the framework we have been developing, numbers are elements of some semantic domain and numerals are elements of some syntactic domain. In the rest of this section, numbers will be written in words. Thus:

```
the numerals:

          1100 in binary
          110 in ternary
          12 in decimal
          C in hexadecimal
          XII in Roman

all represent the number twelve
```

We shall use the normal operator symbols, + and *, to represent addition and multiplication of numbers.

The denotational semantics of the binary numerals is fairly straightforward because there is only one syntactic domain, one semantic domain and one semantic function. The syntactic domain and abstract syntax are shown below.

```
Syntactic Domain

        Bin                 the domain of binary numerals,
                            n is a typical element

Abstract Syntax

        n ::= 0 | 1 | n0 | n1
```

The abstract syntax should be fairly self-explanatory; it tells us how to construct numerals that contain arbitrary numbers of 0s and 1s. The semantic domain is the domain of numbers and our semantic function must map elements of Bin to elements of the semantic domain.

```
Semantic Domain

        Num                 the domain of positive natural
                            numbers and zero

Semantic Function

        N : Bin —> Num
```

The definition of the semantic function uses a standard mathematical notation; the function name appears at the extreme left and is followed by a colon, then follows a definition of the type of the mapping that the function performs. The arrow separates the source domain from the target domain. Thus N is a function mapping the binary numerals to the natural numbers as required. Finally, we must define the function N by specifying the semantic equations.

```
Semantic Equations

        N { 0 } = zero                          (SE.1)
        N { 1 } = one                           (SE.2)
        N { n0 } = two * N { n }                (SE.3)
        N { n1 } = two * N { n } + one          (SE.4)
```

The semantic equations correspond to our intuition of what a binary numeral "means", and N { 0 } can be read as "the meaning of 0". The braces, { and }, are used to delineate syntactic elements in the equations.

We close this introductory section by showing how this denotational description of the binary numerals may be used to prove the correctness of a digitwise addition operator. We shall look at the proof techniques that can be used with denotational semantics in a later section. Many proofs involve the use of some form of inductive method. The proof of a theorem by induction involves two stages; the first stage involves showing that the theorem is true for some initial values, and the second stage involves assuming the theorem true for some arbitrary value and showing that the theorem is true for the next values in some ordering. If we can do this, since our assumption at the second stage was about some arbitrary value, the theorem is true for all possible values. You may be familiar with this technique as the basis for Mathematical Induction which is illustrated below.

```
To prove that:
        1 + 2 + ... + n = n(n+1)/2              for all n

Stage 1, consider n = 1
        LHS     = 1
                = 1(1+1)/2                       Left Hand Side
                = RHS                            Right Hand Side

Stage 2, assume the theorem true for n = k
        Consider n = k + 1
                LHS     = 1 + 2 + ... + k + (k+1)
                        = k(k+1)/2 + (k+1)
                        = (k**2 + 3k + 2)/2
                        = (k+1)(k+2)/2
                        = (k+1)((k+1)+1)/2
                        = RHS
QED
```

Before showing how the technique applies to our correctness proof of the digitwise addition operator, we have to define exactly what the operator does. The operator, represented by #, is commutative, so we only define the necessary cases.

```
0 # n = n           for all n              (BA.1)
1 # 1 = 10                                 (BA.2)
1 # n0 = n1                                (BA.3)
1 # n1 = (n#1)0                            (BA.4)
n0 # m0 = (n#m)0                           (BA.5)
n0 # m1 = (n#m)1                           (BA.6)
n1 # m1 = ((n#m)#1)0                       (BA.7)
```

The juxtaposition of two strings represents their concatenation. We have used brackets in (BA.4) to (BA.7) to indicate that the digitwise additions are performed before the concatenations.

We must prove that the result of performing digitwise addition on two numerals produces the same result as adding the two numbers that they represent, that is:

$$N \{ m \# n \} = N \{ m \} + N \{ n \}$$

The proof involves an induction over the length, that is number of digits, of the second operand. This technique is an example of Structural Induction. The proof starts by considering the cases when the second numeral is only one digit long. Notice that this first stage of the main proof involves a "nested" induction over the length of the first operand.

```
Case 1, n is 0
    Prove:  N { m # 0 } = N { m } + N { 0 }  for all m

        LHS = N { m # 0 }
            = N { m }           by commutativity of # and (BA.1)
            = N { m } + zero
            = N { m } + N { 0 }                      by (SE.1)
            = RHS

Case 2, n is 1
    Prove:  N { m # 1 } = N { m } + N { 1 }  for all m

        Stage 1, consider m is of length 1
            Case 1, m is 0
                LHS = N { 0 # 1 }
                    = N { 1 }       by commutativity and (BA.1)
                    = zero + N { 1 }
                    = N { 0 } + N { 1 }             by (SE.1)
                    = RHS
            Case 2, m is 1
                LHS = N { 1 # 1 }
                    = N { 10 }                   by (BA.2)
                    = two * N { 1 }              by (SE.3)
                    = two * one                  by (SE.2)
                    = one + one
                    = N { 1 } + N { 1 }          by (SE.2)
                    = RHS

        Stage 2, assume true for some arbitrary value of m, say k,
                 and consider the two longer possibilities.
            Case 1, m is k0
                LHS = N { k0 # 1 }
                    = N { k1 }      by commutativity and (BA.3)
                    = two * N { k } + one         by (SE.4)
```

```
                     = N { k0 } + one              by (SE.3)
                     = N { k0 } + N { 1 }          by (SE.2)
                     = RHS
         Case 2, m is k1
              LHS = N { k1 # 1 }
                  = N { (k#1)0 } by commutativity and (BA.4)
                  = two * N { k # 1 }              by (SE.3)
                  = two * ( N { k } + one )    by assumption
                                                   and (SE.2)
                  = ( two * N { k } + one ) + one
                  = N { k1 } + one                 by (SE.4)
                  = N { k1 } + N { 1 }             by (SE.2)
                  = RHS
```

QED

We have now proved the first stage of the main induction. Assuming that the operator is correctly implemented when the second argument has h digits, we now show that the theorem is true when the second argument has (h+1) digits. This proof involves two subcases, for i0 and i1, say (where i has h digits in it). We omit the trivial cases when an operand is 0.

```
SUBCASE 1
To prove that:
    N { m # i0 } = N { m } + N { i0 }  for all m

    N { 1 # i0 } = N { i1 }
                 = two * N { i } + one
                 = N { 1 } + N { i0 }
                 = RHS

    N { j0 + i0 } = N { (j#i)0 }
                  = two * N { j # i }
                  = two * ( N { j } + N { i } ) by our assumption
                  = N { j0 } + N { i0 }
                  = RHS

    N { j1 + i0 } = N { (j#i)1 }
                  = two * N { j # i } + one
                  = two * ( N { j } + N { i } ) + one
                  = two * N { j } + one + N { i0 }
                  = N { j1 } + N { i0 }
                  = RHS
QED

SUBCASE 2
To prove that:
    N { m # i1 } = N { m } + N { i1 }  for all m
```

```
N { 1 # i1 } = N { (1#i)0 }
            = two * N { 1 # i }
            = two * ( one + N { i } )
            = N { 1 } + N { i1 }
            = RHS

N { j0 # i1 } = N { (j#i)1 }
            = two * N { j # i } + one
            = two * ( N { j } + N { i } ) + one
            = two * N { j }  + two * N { i } + one
            = N { j0 } + N { i1 }
            = RHS

N { j1 # i1 } = N { ((j#i)#1)0 }
            = two * N { (j#i)#1 }
            = two * N { j # i } + two
            = two * N { j } + one + two * N { i } + one
            = N { j1 } + N { i1 }
            = RHS
```
QED

That completes our proof of the correctness of the digitwise addition operator and of our treatment of the binary numerals. We now turn our attention to the semantics of SUGAR.

EXERCISES

1. Ternary numerals are constructed from the three digits 0, 1 and 2. Some ternary/decimal equivalents are shown below.

ternary	decimal
1	1
2	2
10	3
11	4
12	5
20	6

Define the denotational semantics of the ternary numerals.

2. A digitwise multiplication operator for binary numerals, @, which is commutative, is defined below:

```
m @ 0 = 0         for all m
m @ 1 = m
m @ n0 = (m @ n)0
m @ n1 = (m @ n)0 # m
```

Prove that:

$$N \{ m @ n \} = N \{ n \} * N \{ m \}$$

6.2 THE SEMANTICS OF SUGAR

As might be expected, the semantics for SUGAR are somewhat more complicated than for the numerals. The mathematical model that we use is an applied λ-calculus rather than the simple number-theoretic model that we used in the last section. First we must decide what the syntactic domains are. We aim to define the meaning of a collection of SUGAR definitions, so we would expect to have a syntactic domain of well-formed definitions. The definitions are constructed from identifiers and expressions, which in turn are constructed from identifiers, constants, operators and lists and alternatives. We have a syntactic domain for each of these categories.

Syntactic Domains

Def	definitions
Exp	expressions
Ide	identifiers
Con	constants
Ops	operators
Lis	lists
Alt	alternatives

In the abstract syntax that follows we use the first letters of the domain names to represent typical elements. Primes (') are used to differentiate elements of the same domain.

Abstract Syntax

```
D ::= I = E | I = E ; D

E ::= E where D |
      C | I | if E then E' A |
      O E | E O E' |
      < L > | <> |
      E ( E' ) | I . E

L ::= E | E , L

A ::= else E endf | elsf E then E' A | endf
```

You should convince yourself that this syntax does faithfully reflect the facilities that are provided in SUGAR. The fifth line of the expression clause provides the syntax for function application and abstraction. We have not included a clause for strings of characters because they are merely a shorthand notation that may be used to represent a list of individual characters.

The semantic domains are shown below.

```
Semantic Domains

        Env              environments
        Bas              basic values
        Prm              primitive operators
        Dev              denotable values
```

The denotable values are the set of values which can be given names in the language. Env, Bas and Dev are not primitive domains, they are constructed from other domains. The rules for domain construction are formally specified in the next section. Env is the domain of environments, an environment being a collection of identifier/value pairs as we defined in the last chapter. Thus it is the domain of mappings from Ide (the syntactic domain of identifiers) to Dev.

```
    Env = Ide -> Dev
```

The literal values that are permissible in SUGAR include integers, real numbers, booleans and characters. Bas is simply the union of these types:

```
    Bas = Int + Real + Char + Bool
```

Finally, there are three types of denotable values in SUGAR, constants, functions and lists, so the Dev domain is constructed from the basic values, the functions that map values into values and the set of lists of values. Lists are denoted as pairs, representing the head and tail of the list, or as "nil", the denotation for the empty list.

```
    Dev = Bas + [ Dev -> Dev ] + {nil} + [ Dev X Dev ]
```

We use the following semantic operators:

⋈   a binary operator that constructs a pair from its operands (NB this is a lazy operation).

head   a unary operator that selects the first element of a pair. It is an error to use head with an operand that is not a pair.

tail   a unary operator that selects the second element of a pair. It is an error to use tail with an operand that is not a pair.

↓   a binary indexing operator. For example:
           list ↓ 3 = head(tail(tail list))

In addition, if an element belongs to a constructed domain, we will require the ability to detect which component of the construction the element is derived from. We will use the following predicates:

boolean   True if the element is from Bool

function   True if the element is from [Dev —> Dev]

list   True if the element is from {nil} + [Dev × Dev]

Hopefully the reader has obtained an intuitive understanding of the domain constructors and associated operations, but, as promised earlier, we will return to a more formal treatment in the next section. We now present the semantic functions for SUGAR.

Semantic Functions

$$
\begin{aligned}
OP &: Ops \longrightarrow Prm \\
CB &: Con \longrightarrow Bas \\
ED &: Exp \longrightarrow Env \longrightarrow Dev \\
LD &: Lis \longrightarrow Env \longrightarrow \{nil\} + [Dev \times Dev] \\
AD &: Alt \longrightarrow Env \longrightarrow Dev \\
DE &: Def \longrightarrow Env \longrightarrow Env
\end{aligned}
$$

The last four functions are shown in their curried form; for example, ED actually needs two parameters, an expression and an environment, before a value can be produced.

We now specify the semantic equations. Most of the operators in SUGAR have a trivial mapping into the semantic domain; the exceptions are the "atom" test and the list operations whose semantics are given below:

$$OP\{ \text{atom} \} = \lambda \text{ x. if list x then false else true} \qquad (OP.1)$$

$$OP\{ \text{hd} \} = \lambda \text{ x. head x} \qquad (OP.2)$$

$$OP\{ \text{tl} \} = \lambda \text{ x. tail x} \qquad (OP.3)$$

$$OP\{ : \} = \lambda \text{ xy. x } \rtimes \text{ y} \qquad (OP.4)$$

$$OP\{ \text{\&\&} \} = \text{fix } \lambda \text{ fxy. if x = nil then y} \qquad (OP.5)$$
$$\text{else (head x) } \rtimes \text{ (f (tail x) y)}$$

The "fix" operator used in (OP.5) finds the fixed points of functions and is equivalent to the "Y" operator of earlier chapters (we define "fix" formally in the next section). The semantic equations for CB trivially map the graphic symbols for constants onto their semantic equivalents and we will not consider them further here. Before presenting the other equations we have to introduce the notation that we will use to represent changes to the environment (cf. the substitution notation used in Chapter 3):

```
if R is a typical element of Env
then R [ x / I ] is the new environment which is the same
                  as R except at I, and I is associated with x
```

The semantic equations for ED, LD, AD and DE are now presented.

Semantic Equations

$$ED\{ \text{ E \textbf{where} D }\}R = ED\{ \text{ E }\} \text{ (DE\{ D }\}R \text{)} \qquad (ED.1)$$

$$ED\{ \text{ C }\}R = CB\{ \text{ C }\} \qquad (ED.2)$$

$$ED\{ \text{ I }\}R = R(\text{ I }) \qquad (ED.3)$$

$$ED\{ \text{ \textbf{if} E \textbf{then} E' A }\}R = \text{ if boolean(} ED\{ \text{ E }\}R \text{)} \qquad (ED.4)$$
$$\text{then if } ED\{ \text{ E }\}R$$
$$\text{then } ED\{ \text{ E' }\}R$$
$$\text{else } AD\{ \text{ A }\}R$$
$$\text{else error}$$

$$ED\{ \text{ O E }\}R = OP\{ \text{ O }\} \text{ } ED\{ \text{ E }\}R \qquad (ED.5)$$

$$ED\{ \text{ E O E' }\}R = OP\{ \text{ O }\} \text{ } ED\{ \text{ E }\}R \text{ } ED\{ \text{ E' }\}R \qquad (ED.6)$$

$$ED\{ \text{ < L > }\}R = LD\{ \text{ L }\}R \qquad (ED.7)$$

$$ED\{ \text{ <> }\}R = \text{nil} \qquad (ED.8)$$

$$ED\{ \ E \ (\ E' \ ) \ \}R \ = \ if \ function(\ ED\{ \ E \ \}R \ )$$
$$then \ ED\{ \ E \ \}R \ ED\{ \ E' \ \}R \qquad (ED.9)$$
$$else \ if \ list(\ ED\{ \ E \ \}R \ )$$
$$then \ ED\{ \ E \ \}R \ \downarrow \ ED\{ \ E' \ \}R$$
$$else \ error$$

$$ED\{ \ I \ . \ E \ \}R \ = \ \lambda x.ED\{ \ E \ \}R[\ x \ / \ I \ ] \qquad (ED.10)$$

$$LD\{ \ E \ \}R \ = \ ED\{ \ E \ \}R \ \vdash \ nil \qquad (LD.1)$$

$$LD\{ \ E \ , \ L \ \}R \ = \ ED\{ \ E \ \}R \ \vdash \ LD\{ \ L \ \}R \qquad (LD.2)$$

$$AD\{ \ \textbf{else} \ E \ \textbf{endf} \ \}R \ = \ ED\{ \ E \ \}R \qquad (AD.1)$$

$$AD\{ \ \textbf{elsf} \ E \ \textbf{then} \ E' \ A \ \}R \ = \ ED\{ \ if \ E \ \textbf{then} \ E' \ A\}R \qquad (AD.2)$$

$$AD\{ \ \textbf{endf} \ \}R \ = \ error \qquad (AD.3)$$

$$DE\{ \ I \ = \ E \ \}R$$
$$= \ R[\ fix(\ \lambda X. \ ED\{ \ E \ \}R[\ X \ / \ I \ ] \ ) \ / \ I \ ] \qquad (DE.1)$$

$$DE\{ \ I \ = \ E; \ D \ \}R$$
$$= \ DE\{ \ D \ \}R[\ fix(\ \lambda X.ED\{ \ E \ \} \ (DE\{ \ D \ \} \ R[X/I]) \ ) \ /I] \qquad (DE.2)$$

(ED.1) says that the environment must be updated with any auxiliary definitions before an expression is evaluated.

(ED.2) to (ED.8) should be self-explanatory and we will not deal with them further in this section.

(ED.9) tells us that in a function application both the function and its parameter should be evaluated in the same environment before the application is performed. The abstract syntax only allows for curried application of functions. If a list is applied to an expression then the $\downarrow$ operator is used to select the appropriate value.

(ED.10) shows how functions are mapped into λ-expressions, the bound variable of the SUGAR function changing to x, the first available variable name.

(LD.1), (LD.2) and (AD.1) to (AD.3) are straightforward.

The semantics of definitions need some careful thought. (DE.1) caters for single definitions. The meaning of a definition is that the environment is updated with the value of the expression on the right hand side of the equals sign. It would be tempting to write:

$$DE\{ \ I \ = \ E \ \}R \ = \ R[\ ED\{ \ E \ \}R \ / \ I \ ] \qquad (DE.1')$$

Unfortunately, this is not correct, because the definition may be recursive. You will remember from Chapter 3 that we removed recursion by abstracting out the name of the function and then using a fixed point operator, and this is exactly what (DE.1) does.

A first attempt at defining the semantics of a pair of definitions separated by semi-colons might be:

DE[I = E; D]R = DE[D](DE[I = E]R)   (DE.2')

In other words, the second definition should be evaluated in the environment created by the first definition. However, this enforces an ordered interpretation of a program which is not correct; in particular it does not cater for the possibility that the definitions are mutually recursive. In fact the semantics of a list of definitions is:

DE[I = E; D]R = DE[D](DE[I = E](DE[D] ...   (DE.2")

This is represented by the fixed point expression in (DE.2).

The use of the semantic equations and in particular (DE.2) can best be illustrated by an example. The following gives the semantics of a simple SUGAR program.

```
SUGAR:
        a is 2;
        b is a;

Semantics:
 => DE[ a = 2; b = a ]R

 => DE[b=a] R[ fix( λX. ED[2] (DE[b=a] R[X/a]) ) / a ] by (DE.2)

 => DE[b=a] R[ fix( λX. CB[2] ) / a ]                      by (ED.2)

 => DE[b=a] R[ fix( λX. 2 ) / a ]

 => DE[b=a] R[ 2 / a ]

 => R[2/a] [ fix( λX. ED[a] R[2/a][X/b] ) / b ]       by (DE.1)

 => R[2/a] [ fix( λX. 2 ) / b ]                           by (ED.2)

 => R[2/a][2/b]
```

Thus the meaning of the program is an environment in which both a and b are associated with 2.

Assuming that we use normal order reduction when interpreting λ-expressions, the semantics that we have defined corresponds to call-by-name semantics. (In fact by using the lazy operator $\rtimes$ we have specified semantics that corresponds to lazy evaluation.) We could change our interpretation so that the semantics of an abstraction is a strict function whose value is undefined if any of its parameters are undefined: we would then have call-by-value semantics.

That completes our treatment of the denotational semantics of SUGAR. We now turn our attention to the mathematical foundations of the notation.

EXERCISE

1. Modify the semantics of SUGAR to provide call-by-value parameter passing.

6.3 MATHEMATICAL FOUNDATIONS

We start by discussing why it is necessary to restrict the sets that we use as domains in our semantics. There are two features of our notation which are problematical. The first is that we rely heavily on recursive definitions of functions and assume the existence of fixed points. The second is that we have had to define recursive domains but we have no guarantee of the existence of such objects.

The first problem is illustrated by the syntactically correct SUGAR definition shown below:

```
f is [ x ] f(x) + 1;
```

The semantics of this definition can be derived by using semantic equation (DE.1):

```
DE{ f = x.f(x) + 1 }R
= R[ fix(λX.ED{ x.f(x) + 1 }R[X/f]) / f ]
= R[ fix(λX.λy.ED{ X(x) + 1 }R[y/x]) / f ]
= R[ fix(λX.λy. + X(y) 1) / f ]
```

However, if we do not restrict our domains and we apply the techniques of Section 3.4 to evaluate the fixed point, we find that it does not exist (we get a non-terminating sequence of reductions) and thus the semantics tells us nothing about the meaning of the definition. This is extremely undesirable because a formal semantics should tell us exactly what the meaning is in any circumstance.

To illustrate the second problem we consider the definition of the domain of denotable values, Dev, which we gave earlier:

$$\texttt{Dev = Bas + [Dev -> Dev] + \{nil\} + [Dev} \times \texttt{Dev]}$$

If we use unrestricted sets and functions then there is no set that satisfies the above definition. This is because for any set Dev, the set of functions defined on that set will always contain many more elements and thus the definition is paradoxical. (Just consider the set of functions that map elements of the domain into $\{0,1\}$ (a very small subset of the functions that we could define). For each element we have two choices for the mapping and thus we can define 2^n distinct functions if there are n elements in the domain. For any reasonable size of n, 2^n is much bigger than n.)

The solution to both of these problems, discussed in the rest of this section, consists of imposing a structure, a partial ordering, on the sets and by constraining functions to preserve the structure. In fact we only require the range of a function to have an isomorphic structure to its domain. The imposition of the correct structure ensures that recursively defined domains exist and that all recursive functions have at least one fixed point.

An essential notion involved in the structuring of sets is the concept of approximations. Approximations are concerned with the information content of elements in a set. We say that an element x of a set approximates another element, y, if y contains at least all of the information that is in x. The fact that one element approximates another is represented by the following notation:

$$x \leq y \qquad \qquad \texttt{x approximates y}$$

The approximates relation will be defined differently for different domains. For example, in the domain of sets it might well be the set inclusion relation. An example will serve to clarify this idea; considering the non-empty subsets of $\{1,2,3\}$, some of the approximations (based on set inclusion) are shown below:

$$\{1\} \leq \{1,2\}$$
$$\{1\} \leq \{1,3\}$$
$$\{2\} \leq \{1,2\}$$
$$\{1,2\} \leq \{1,2,3\}$$

The structure of a domain is often shown graphically, giving a far clearer picture of the approximates relation.

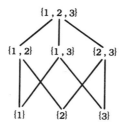

An arc in the graph represents the fact that the element at the lower end of the arc approximates the element at the top. Elements that contain incompatible information are incomparable so, for example, there is no arc between {1,3} and {2,3}.

Our domains are structured such that every domain contains an element that is totally undefined, sometimes written as $\perp$ (bottom). This element approximates every other element in the domain. Any sequence in which each element approximates to the next is called a directed sequence. An additional constraint on the structure of our domains is that any directed sequence must converge to a well-behaved limit. For example, the limit of the sequence $\perp$, {1}, {1,2}, {1,2,3} is {1,2,3}. Any function that we define on our domains must preserve these limits or, more formally, we only allow continuous functions. A function is defined to be continuous if it satisfies the following condition.

```
f : D —> D' is continuous if and only if,
for any directed sequence X in D :
        f(lub X) = lub { f(x) such that x ε X }
```

The term "lub" stands for "least upper bound" and is the limit to which the sequence converges. In words, the constraint may be interpreted to mean that a function is continuous if the result of applying it to the limit of a sequence is equal to the limit of the sequence generated when it is applied to the individual elements of the original sequence.

Continuous functions defined on our domains are also monotonic; the condition for monotonicity is given below:

```
f is monotonic if whenever  x ≤ y , f(x) ≤ f(y)
```

Primitive sets in which all the elements are incomparable can be turned into domains by simply adding a bottom element. The longest directed sequence in such a domain contains two elements: bottom and any other element.

There are several ways that we can construct non-primitive domains and these are illustrated below:

(1)   The product domain, $D_1 \times D_2$

         set of ordered pairs (d_1,d_2) where $d_1 \epsilon D_1$ and $d_2 \epsilon D_2$
         $(d_1,d_2) \le (d_1',d_2')$
         if $d_1 \le d_1'$ and $d_2 \le d_2'$
         bottom is $(\perp_1,\perp_2)$

(2)   The sum domain, $D_1 + D_2$

         set of elements from either D_1 or D_2
         elements from different domains are incomparable
         $\perp_1$ and $\perp_2$ are both elements of $D_1 + D_2$ and
         there is a new bottom that approximates both

(3)   The domain of continuous functions, $D_1 \rightarrow D_2$

         $f \le g$ if for all $x \epsilon D_1$ $f(x) \le g(x)$
         bottom is the function that is everywhere undefined

(4)   The domain of lists of length n, D^n

         $D^n = D \times D \times \ldots D$
         $d \le d'$ if each element in d approximates the
         corresponding element in d'
         bottom is $(\perp,\perp,\ldots,\perp)$

(5)   The domain of finite lists, D^*

         $D^* = D^0 + D^1 + \ldots$
         lists of different lengths are incomparable
         there is a new bottom that approximates all the others

These different domain constructors may be combined to produce more and more complex domain definitions. In a definition that contains several different constructors, the unary constructors have highest priority, followed by $\times$, $+$ and $\rightarrow$. The priorities may be overridden by using square brackets. There is an alternative definition of the sum constructor, called a coalesced sum, which does not contain the bottom elements of the summand domains but has a single bottom element.

Finally we look at the definition of the "fix" function that was used in Section 6.2. The functionality of fix is shown below:

      fix : [$D \rightarrow D$] $\rightarrow$ D   where D is some domain

Thus fix takes an arbitrary continuous function on some domain and produces its fixed point. The definition of fix depends crucially on the notions of approximation, monotonicity and continuity. Firstly, because D is a domain and therefore bottom approximates everything else, we get the following approximation:

$$\perp \leq f(\perp)$$

Then as f is monotonic, we can apply f to both sides of the approximation to get:

$$f(\perp) \leq f^2(\perp) \text{ where } f^2(\perp) = f(f(\perp))$$

This process can be continued indefinitely and, in doing so, a sequence of approximations is constructed. As we are dealing with a continuous function on a domain, this sequence is guaranteed to have a limit:

$$\lim_{n \Rightarrow \infty} f^n(\perp) = \text{lub } f^n(\perp)$$

The final step is to look at what happens when f is applied to this limit. Again, because f is continuous, we get the following sequence of equalities:

$$
\begin{aligned}
f(\text{lub } f^n(\perp)) &= \text{lub } f(f^n(\perp)) \\
&= \text{lub } f^{n+1}(\perp) \\
&= \text{lub } f^n(\perp)
\end{aligned}
$$

Thus the limit of the sequence is a fixed point of the function; but is it the one that we want? In cases where a function has a number of different fixed points, we are interested in the fixed point that contains the least information, the so-called minimal or least fixed point. It is quite easy to show that if there are other fixed points they will contain more information than the one that we have just derived:

Suppose there is another fixed point, say y, then:

$$\perp \leq y \qquad \text{by definition}$$

$$\text{therefore } f(\perp) \leq f(y) = y \qquad \text{because f is monotonic}$$

repeating this process:

$$\text{lub } f^n(\perp) \leq y$$

Therefore we define fix to be the limit:

```
fix = λf. lub fⁿ( ⊥ )
```

That completes our brief excursion into the mathematical foundations of the notation and sets the scene for a description of some of the proof techniques that can be used. A more rigorous and complete treatment of the material can be found in Stoy [Sto].

6.4 PROOF TECHNIQUES

There are several different techniques that may be used to prove properties of programs. We do not attempt to give an exhaustive description of these techniques in this book. Three methods that we shall look at briefly are Structural Induction, the Minimal Fixed Point Property and Fixed Point Induction. However, first we show how to use the techniques of the last section to find the least fixed point of a function.

6.4.1 Finding Fixed Points

The proof techniques that we present in the next three sections seldom involve the evaluation of a fixed point. However, for completeness, we illustrate how fixed points may be found using the technique that was used to motivate the definition of fix in the last section. We start with a simple example and then proceed to a more complicated one. The technique that is used involves constructing a sequence of approximations to the fixed point, $f(\bot)$, $f^2(\bot)$ ..., and taking the limit of the sequence.

First we consider the factorial function, which has the semantics shown below

```
f  = fix F
        where F = λ Xx. if = x 0 then 1 else * x X(− x 1)
```

The sequence of approximations starts as shown below:

```
F(⊥) = λx. if = x 0 then 1 else * x ⊥(− x 1)
F(⊥) = λx. if = x 0 then 1 else ⊥
```

```
F²(⊥) = λx. if = x 0 then 1 else * x F(⊥)(− x 1)
F²(⊥) = λx. if = x 0 then 1 else
                 if = x 1 then x else ⊥
        .
        .
        .
```

The limit of this sequence is the infinite conditional expression:

```
λ x. if x = 0 then 1
        else if x = 1 then x
        else if x = 2 then x * (x − 1)
        .
        .
        .
```

which is clearly the factorial function.

The second example is a function that constructs an infinite list of integers and is represented by the following SUGAR definition and semantics:

```
SUGAR:
        f is [n] n : f(n + 1);

Semantics:
        f = fix F
                where F = λ Xx. x ⊢ X( + x 1)
```

The sequence generated in this case is:

```
F(⊥) = λ x. x ⊢ ⊥(+ x 1)
F²(⊥) = λ x. x ⊢ (λ x. x ⊢ ⊥(+ x 1))(+ x 1)
        .
        .
        .
```

It is important to notice that ⊢ is lazy, so no simplification takes place in the right hand operand. However, it is clear that the sequence is converging to a lazy representation of:

```
λx. < x , < x + 1, < x + 2, ...
```

as required. We now turn our attention to a description of the three proof techniques mentioned in the introduction to this section.

6.4.2 Structural Induction

To prove that a property holds over a domain using structural induction involves two stages. Firstly, the property is shown to hold for all atomic elements and, secondly, it is shown that each constructor defined in the domain preserves the property. This means that for non-atomic elements we use the inductive hypothesis that the property holds for the proper subcomponents of the construct. We have already seen an example of structural induction in the proof of correctness of the digitwise addition operator. The property that we needed to prove was:

```
N{ m # n } = N{ m } + N{ n }      for all m and n
```

We did this by proving the equality for each possible form that m and n could take. In the cases where m and n were complex, we assumed that the equality held for all shorter strings of digits.

6.4.3 The Minimal Fixed Point Property

This technique is used to prove that two functions have the same minimal fixed point. The proof involves showing that the least fixed point of each function is also a fixed point of the other:

```
Consider two functions f and g :

if fix g is a fixed point of f, then fix f ≤ fix g

if fix f is a fixed point of g, then fix g ≤ fix f

if both of the above conditions hold then fix f = fix g
```

As an example of this technique we prove the equivalence of a tail recursive definition of a function to add a sequence of integers to the corresponding "divide and conquer" definition. A divide and conquer algorithm is one that splits a task up into a binary tree of sub-tasks, a very useful approach to take in a parallel processing environment. The two functions that we shall use are shown below:

```
F is [ n,m ] if n = m then m
             else n + F(n+1, m)
             endf ;

G is [ n,m ] if n = m then m
             else G(n,(n+m)%2) + G((n+m)%2+1,m)
             endf ;
```

The semantics of these two SUGAR definitions, using infix semantic operators, are given by the following equations:

```
          F = fix f
where
          f = λX.λxy. if x = y then y else x + X(x+1,y)

          G = fix g
where
          g = λX.λxy. if x = y then y else X(x,k) + X(k+1,y)

          and k is the midpoint of x and y
```

Thus in order to prove that F and G are equivalent, we have to prove that f and g have the same minimal fixed point. We use the minimal fixed point property to do this; in this section we only prove that fix f is also a fixed point of g. The other half of the proof, which is very similar, is left as an exercise for the reader.

```
We need to prove that:

          g(fix f) = fix f

Now       g(fix f) = λxy. if x = y then y
                              else (fix f)(x,k) + (fix f)(k+1,y)

and by the definition of f, we get:

f(fix f) = fix f = λxy. if x = y then y else x + (fix f)(x+1,y)
```

We can use numerical induction over the difference between x and y in order to prove the equality.

```
if x = y :

          g(fix f)(x,y) = y
                        = (fix f)(x,y)

assume that the equality holds for all values of y
such that y − x < n.

consider the case when y = x + n :

g(fix f)(x,y) = (fix f)(x,k) + (fix f)(k+1,y)          by definition
              = x + (fix f)(x+1,k) + (fix f)(k+1,y)    by definition
              = x + (fix f)(x+1,y)                     by hypothesis
              = (fix f)(x,y)                           by definition
```

6.4.4 Fixed Point Induction

The method of fixed point induction may be used to show that a certain property, P, holds for the least fixed point of a function. A proof using fixed point induction proceeds by showing that the property holds for the bottom element, and assuming that it holds for some arbitrary X, proving that it holds for $f(X)$. This process can be summarized as shown below:

```
To show that property P holds for fix f :

    (1) Prove P(⊥)
    (2) Assuming P(X), prove P(f(X))
```

Unfortunately, fixed point induction cannot be used to prove all properties. Using a normal inductive argument about the parameter of P, the above process proves that P holds for the directed sequence $\bot, f(\bot)...f^m(\bot)$ for all n. We want to infer from this that P also holds for the least upper bound of the sequence (which is the least fixed point of f) but we can only do this if P is inclusive:

```
A predicate P is inclusive if :

    ∧ { P(x) such that x ∈ X } => P ( lub X )
                        when X is directed
```

$\wedge$ produces the conjunction of the elements of the set and $\Longrightarrow$ is logical implication. Tests for equality and approximation between continuous functions are two examples of useful inclusive properties.

We illustrate the use of fixed point induction giving an example based on the following SUGAR function:

```
length is [x] if x = <> then 0 else length(tl(x))+1 endf;
```

We shall prove the following property:

```
length ( x && y ) = length ( x ) + length ( y )
```

The semantics of SUGAR gives length the following meaning:

```
length = fix f
        where f = λ Xx. if x = <> then 0 else X(tl(x)) + 1
```

We have used infix operators to make the equation easier to read as we did in the previous example. The property P is defined as shown below:

```
P(F) = ( F(x&&y) = F(x) + F(y) ) &
       ( F(x:y) = 1 + F(y) )  &
       ( F(<>) + F(y) = F(y) )
```

The first part is the property that we want to prove, the second two parts are needed in the proof of the first part. The second part tells us that the length of a list is one greater than the length of the tail of the list and the third part tells us that the length of the empty list is 0. We could not use the simpler:

```
F(<>) = 0
```

since this does not hold for bottom. We now present the proof:

Basis :

```
⊥(x&&y) = ⊥ = ⊥(x) + ⊥(y)
⊥(x:y) = ⊥ = 1 + ⊥(y)
⊥(<>) + ⊥(y) = ⊥ = ⊥(y)                    By properties of ⊥
```

Hypothesis :

```
(L(x&&y) = L(x) + L(y)) & (L(x:y) = 1 + L(y)) &
(L(<>) + L(y) = L(y))
```

Induction :

```
(i) f(L)(x) + f(L)(y)
        = (if x = <> then 0 else L(tl(x)) + 1) +
          (if y = <> then 0 else L(tl(y)) + 1)    By definition

        = if x = <> & y = <> then 0
          elsf y = <> then L(tl(x)) + 1
          elsf x = <> then L(tl(y)) + 1
          else L(tl(x)) + 1 + L(tl(y)) + 1

        = if x = <> & y = <> then 0
          elsf y = <> then L(tl(x)) + 1
          elsf x = <> then L(tl(y)) + 1
          else L(tl(x)) + 1 + L(y)           By hypothesis (ii)

        = if x&&y = <> then 0
          elsf y = <> then L(tl(x&&y)) + 1
          elsf x = <> then L(tl(x&&y)) + 1
          else L(tl(x&&y)) + 1               By hypothesis (i)
                                             and definition of &&

        = if x&&y = <> then 0
          else L(tl(x&&y)) + 1
        = f(L)(x&&y)
```

```
(ii) f(L)(x:y)
          = if x:y = <> then 0 else L(y) + 1          By definition

          = L(y) + 1                                  By definition of ":"

     1 + f(L)(y)
          = 1 + if y = <> then 0 else L(tl(y)) + 1

          = 1 + if y = <> then 0 else L(y)       By hypothesis (ii)

          = 1 + if y = <> then L(<>) else L(y) By hypothesis(iii)

          = 1 + L(y)


(iii) f(L)(<>) + f(L)(y)
          = (if <> = <> then 0 else L(tl(<>)) + 1) + f(L)(y)
                                                    By definition

          = 0 + f(L)(y)

          = f(L)(y)
```

Further examples may be found in Manna et al. [Man] and Stoy [Sto].

EXERCISES

1. Complete the proof of Section 6.4.3, i.e. prove:

   ```
   fix f ≤ fix g
   ```


2. Find the minimal fixed point of:

   ```
   f is [x] if x > 43 then 42 else f(x+1) endf;
   ```


3. Find the minimal fixed point of:

   ```
   f is [x] f(x) + 1;
   ```

where $+$ is a strict operator.

4. Use the methods of the last section to show that:

```
f is [x] if x > 100 then x - 10
          else f ( f ( x + 11 ))
          endf;
```

has the same minimal fixed point as:

```
f is [x] if x > 100 then x - 10 else 91 endf;
```

BIBLIOGRAPHY

There are two excellent books devoted to the subject matter of this chapter. Gordon is a non-mathematical overview of the Scott-Strachey approach, while Stoy gives a rigorous treatment of the subject with many examples and exercises. There is also a chapter by Stoy in Darlington et al. which gives a readable overview of Scott's latest work on the mathematical foundations. The paper by Tennent provides a tutorial introduction to denotational semantics with a large example at the end. Manna et al. is a seminal paper on program proving techniques. Pagan gives a very readable description of various formal definition techniques.

[Dar] Darlington J., Henderson P. and Turner D.A. "Functional Programming and its Applications", Cambridge University Press, 1982.

[Gor] Gordon M.J.C. "The Denotational Description of Programming Languages", Springer-Verlag, 1979.

[Man] Manna Z., Ness S. and Vuillemin J. "Inductive Methods for Proving Properties of Programs", Communications of the ACM, Vol. 16, No. 8, August 1973.

[Pag] Pagan F.G. "Formal Specification of Programming Languages", Prentice-Hall, 1981.

[Sto] Stoy J.E. "Denotational Semantics: The Scott-Strachey Approach to Programming Language Theory", MIT Press, 1977.

[Te2] Tennent R.D. "The Denotational Semantics of Programming Languages", Communications of the ACM, Vol. 19, No. 8, August 1976.

PART 3

THE FUNCTIONAL LANGUAGE LANDSCAPE

The language SUGAR which we have used to demonstrate the central concepts of functional programming is a rather minimal language of its kind; indeed it is hardly more than an applied λ-calculus with an improved syntactic form. In this final part of the book, we are going to look at functional languages other than SUGAR. We look at the language that was the first functional language to become generally available, we review some more recent languages and the important additional features which they embrace, and we try to discern what might be the directions for progress in the future.

So first we look at LISP, a language which has been with us for more than twenty years, perhaps the only functional language which is known to those not working in the field. We shall see that though superficially it does seem to provide function definition facilities based upon the λ-calculus, nevertheless it contains various impurities which are quite at variance with the functional style, such as assignments, jumps, the identification of data and function descriptions, call-by-value parameters and dynamic binding of names. However, quite apart from its historical interest, we feel that it is worth devoting some time to a study of the language, since some of its impurities can be used to throw into relief the properties of a pure functional system. It was also in our minds that there may be readers who only have access to a LISP system, and so we shall see that it is possible, though not very desirable, to use a subset of LISP in order to write functional programs.

Next we look at some of the more recent languages, and the important new features which they contain. One of the most significant concepts missing from SUGAR is data abstraction, that is, the ability to define structured data aggregates, and the necessary operations on those aggregates. When we have the ability to distinguish many different types of data object, it is natural to want type checking to be done at syntax analysis time, in order to pick up errors which involve the application of operations to inappropriate objects. In a sense, the introduction of type checking implies a restriction on the programmer's freedom, in the interests of more reliable program production. We might go on to ask whether it is desirable to restrict the programmer in other ways; for example, one restriction which has been contemplated is a limitation on the freedom to define higher order functions, on the basis that they are conceptually difficult to handle, and can give rise to obscure programs.

Finally, we try to look to the future of functional programming, for example, the attempt to apply functional programming techniques to operating system design, and we look at one of the other directions of language design currently being pursued, the development of logic programming languages, discussing its relationship to functional programming.

7

FUNCTIONAL PROGRAMMING IN LISP

The language LISP was designed by John McCarthy in the early sixties. He wanted a language whose basic concepts were mathematical in nature, so that it could draw on the theory of recursive functions which had been developed over the previous twenty or thirty years. He also wanted a language which would be suitable for non-numerical applications, and so powerful list-processing facilities were included. He was particularly interested in applications in artificial intelligence; over the years since it became available, extensive use has indeed been made of LISP in this field, especially in the United States. However, in order to ensure that programs in the language ran at an acceptable speed, and perhaps because the idea of a functional programming language was just too unfamiliar at that time, features were put into the language which destroyed its simplicity of design. These features, given full rein, make the language rather like an imperative language, but with very inconvenient syntax. Thus there are really two LISPs: the functional core and the extended language, which includes such features as explicit jumps, labels and assignments.

We are going to describe a particular small functional subset of LISP, which we shall call FLISP. This will entail some considerable simplification of the language. The flow of control features have naturally been excised, but so have certain other features which would not of themselves destroy the functional nature of the language, in order that FLISP should be a minimal functional language in the same way that SUGAR is minimal. It is intended that this subset can be used to run programs on any implementation of LISP which the reader has available. This will mean that we have to adopt some of the conventions of any particular implementation, but FLISP is designed to be insensitive to semantic peculiarities of implementations, assuming that certain central concepts in LISP are handled in the standard way. For anyone wishing to know more about LISP in its full form, there are several books which can be consulted (see the bibliography). However, we advise that the reader should understand our presentation of FLISP first, since those books, with the exception of Henderson [Hen], are concerned to make LISP seem attractive to programmers who are more familiar with conventional languages, and tend to obscure the simplicity of the functional core of the language. Henderson, on the other hand, uses a variant of LISP as a means of writing programs in the functional style. Whereas we have tried to use LISP systems as they are, he designs and implements a variant which eliminates some of the problems which arise out of basic concepts of LISP, and also the problems which come about because implementors have departed from basic concepts in different ways.

7.1 FLISP, A FUNCTIONAL SUBSET OF LISP

An FLISP program is a sequence of function definitions and function applications. The building bricks from which larger grammatical units are constructed are called atoms; atoms are strings of characters, some representing integers and possibly real numbers, some having special significance within the language, and some which may be used as identifiers. The only construction mechanism for creating more complex structures from more primitive ones is the bracketed sequence; given some already constructed units, say $unit_1$, $unit_2$, ... $unit_n$, we may form the new unit

        (unit$_1$ unit$_2$ ... unit$_n$)

In particular, the application of a function, say fn, to a set of arguments, say arg_1, arg_2, ... arg_n is represented by

        (fn arg$_1$ arg$_2$ ... arg$_n$)

There follows an example of a program, using the conventions of a LISP system available to the authors; some of the grammatical units of which the program is composed are also displayed; note that the commas used here are to separate similar units, and are not part of FLISP:

```
program:
        (def dub (lambda (x) (plus x x)))
        (mapcar (quote dub) (quote (1 3 5 7 9)))
        (exit)

atoms:
        def, lambda, quote, plus, mapcar, exit,
        dub, x, 1, 3, 5, 7, 9

bracketed sequences:
        (plus x x), (lambda (x) (plus x x)),
        (def dub (lambda (x) (plus x x))),
        (1 3 5 7 9), (quote (1 3 5 7 9)),
        (quote dub), (mapcar (quote dub) (quote (1 3 5 7 9))),
        (exit)

function definition:
        (def dub (lambda (x) (plus x x)))

function applications:
        (mapcar (quote dub) (quote (1 3 5 7 9))),
        (plus x x)
```

Note that function definitions and function applications are also bracketed sequences. A function definition is recognized as such because the first element is the symbol "def"; similarly, a function description is introduced by the symbol "lambda". The bracketed sequence "(exit)" is used to indicate that no more computation is required.

We have been rather informal about the syntactic structure of the language, but we will need to be quite precise about this, and so we are going to give a formal specification of the form of FLISP programs; the names introduced here to represent syntactic units will be used in the remainder of this chapter to refer to examples of those units, and so we also give the correspondence between the informal terms we have used until now, and the more formal terms we shall use henceforth:

FLISP syntax

```
        Program      ::=  { Defn | Elem }  Terminator
        Defn         ::=  ( def  Id  Lambdaexp )
        Lambdaexp    ::=  ( lambda  Args  Body )
        Body         ::=  Elem
        Args         ::=  ( { Id } )
        Brack        ::=  ( { Elem } ) | nil
        Elem         ::=  Brack | Atom
        Atom         ::=  Id | Num | Quotedcharstring | nil
```

Note that:

braces are used to mean zero or more occurrences of whatever they enclose.

the Ids of Defns must be distinct from any system-defined Ids; the Ids of Args must be distinct from system-defined Ids, and from Ids of Defns.

The correspondences between the names used here for syntactic units, and our more informal terminology are:

```
Program        program;
Defn           function definition;
Lambdaexp      function description;
Args           list of names of parameters of a function
                   description;
Body           the body of a function description;
Atom           atom;
Brack          bracketed sequence;
Elem           atom or bracketed sequence;
Id             the name of a function, variable
                   or system-defined entity;
Num            an atom representing an integer or real number;
Quotedcharstring
               an atom representing a string of characters;
Terminator     indication that program text is finished.
```

Now we illustrate the meanings of the formal names of syntactic units by taking a second look at the program we gave earlier:

```
Program:
        (def dub (lambda (x) (plus x x)))
        (mapcar (quote dub) (quote (1 3 5 7 9)))
        (exit)

Defn:
        (def dub (lambda (x) (plus x x)))

Lambdaexp:
        (lambda (x) (plus x x))

Body:
        (plus x x)

Args:
        (x)
```

Bracks:

    (plus x x), (1 3 5 7 9), (quote (1 3 5 7 9)),
    (quote dub), (mapcar (quote dub) (quote (1 3 5 7 9)))

Elems:

    x, 1, (plus x x), (quote dub), etc.

Atoms:

    def, lambda, quote, plus, mapcar,
    dub, x,
    1, 3, 5, 7, 9

Ids:

    quote, plus, mapcar, x, dub

Nums:

    1, 3, 5, 7, 9

Note that:

a unit of the form (def ...) at Program level will always be treated as a Defn even though it looks like a Brack; at an inner level it would fail to evaluate, according to FLISP semantics.

though (lambda (x) (plus x x)) also looks like a Brack, and indeed could be a Brack in another Program, here it is a Lambdaexp because of its context.

Since we want to be able to execute FLISP programs on whatever LISP system is available, we will have to adopt the conventions of that system. The differences between systems are both at the level of trivial syntactic detail and, more significantly, in their semantics.

At the level of syntactic detail, implementations may differ with regard to the characters which may form Ids, the basic types of objects, the names of the system-defined Atoms, the format of Defns, and the convention for comments. We will assume that Ids may consist of a letter, upper or lower case, followed by any number of letters or digits; that a Num consists of a sequence of decimal digits; that a Quotedcharstring consists of a sequence of characters enclosed by quotation marks ("); and that layout characters may be used freely for the sake of clarity, and in order to separate Atoms where necessary. We will adopt the convention that comments may be put on any line which begins with "//". The Program Terminator will depend on the operating system on which the LISP system runs: it is often possible to use a single control character in order to exit from the LISP system, but we will write "(exit)", which as its form implies is really the invocation of a special function "exit", without parameters, which has the effect of returning from the LISP system.

At the semantic level, some interpreters expect to be given one Elem or Defn at a time to be evaluated, whereas others expect a pair consisting of a function and a set of arguments for that function; FLISP adopts the first of these two approaches, because we feel that the second is rather inconsistent, entailing a different notation for function application at the Program level compared with that at all other levels of nesting. Even more importantly, from the semantic point of view, interpreters differ in the facilities they provide for the association of names with values; we shall show how it is possible to write FLISP programs so that they are not sensitive to this aspect of a given interpreter. Again at the semantic level, implementations differ in their willingness to force an Elem to deliver a function when needed, but the problem, if it arises, can be overcome by explicitly forcing evaluation.

As we have already mentioned, certain Atoms have special significance in the language; most of these are simply system-defined functions, such as "plus" and "mapcar" (we will give a more complete list later), but a certain small set of Atoms are called "special forms" because they do not act like functions. Before we can describe what it means to execute an FLISP Program, we need to introduce these special forms:

Special Forms

```
def      introduces a Defn.

lambda introduces a Lambdaexp.

quote  is used to shield an Elem from immediate evaluation.
```

cond   gives the effect of conditional evaluation as described in the semantics below; the format of a Brack introduced by cond is (cond ($(Elem_{1a}\ Elem_{1b})$ $(Elem_{2a}\ Elem_{2b})$ ...
$(Elem_{na}\ Elem_{nb})$)), where $Elem_{na}$ is the special form t.

nil   is an Atom whose associated value is always nil, and is semantically equivalent to the empty Brack, ( ); also has the significance "false" when that is meaningful.

t   is an Atom whose associated value is always t, and has significance "true" when that is meaningful.

In many LISP implementations there is a shorthand notation for quote;

for example, it is often possible to write 'Elem instead of (quote Elem), which has the distinct advantage of removing one level of bracketing. We shall not use any such notation here, but this is only because we want the use of quote to be seen very clearly on the page.

We now describe informally how an FLISP Program is executed:

FLISP semantics

```
execute a Program:-
        evaluate in turn the Defns and Elems of which it is
        composed, printing out the values of the Elems.
- - - -
evaluate a Defn:-
        associate the Lambdaexp with the Id, so that the Id may
        henceforth be used as a name for the function which that
        Lambdaexp describes.
- - - -
evaluate an Elem:-
        when an Atom, deliver the value of the Atom;
        when a Brack, whose first Elem is quote,
            deliver the second Elem as it is;
        when a Brack, whose first Elem is cond,
            deliver the result of conditional evaluation of the
            second Elem of the Brack;
        when a Brack, whose first Elem is an Id,
            whose association is a function description,
            deliver the result of invoking that function with the
            remaining Elems of the Brack as its parameters;
        when a Brack, whose first Elem is a Lambdaexp,
            deliver the result of invoking the function which
            that Lambdaexp represents, with the remaining Elems of
            the Brack as its parameters;
        otherwise evaluation fails.
- - - -
conditional evaluation of a Brack:-
        when the Brack is of the form described in the preceding
            table, evaluate the first Elem of each Elem of
            the Brack in order, until one of these delivers t, and
            then deliver the value of the second Elem of that Elem;
        otherwise, evaluation fails.
- - - -
invoke a function with Elems as its parameters:-
        when the number of Elems corresponds to the number of Ids of
            the Args of the function, evaluate each of those Elems,
            and then having associated the values obtained with
            those Ids in the corresponding order, overriding any
            existing associations for those Ids for the duration of
            this invocation, evaluate the Body of the function;
        otherwise, invocation fails.
```

```
- - - -
the value of an Atom:-
      when the Id of a Defn, is nil;
      when an Id of the Args of a function, is the association for
          that Id currently in force;
      when a Num, is the number it represents;
      when a Quotedcharstring, is the string consisting of the
          quoted characters;
      when nil, is nil, with significance "false" when appropriate;
      when t, is t, with significance "true" when appropriate.
- - - -
```

It will be seen from this description of semantics that the parameter passing mechanism is basically call-by-value, but by using the special form "quote", the evaluation of a parameter can be delayed, and by use of the system-defined function "eval" the value of that parameter can be computed when or if it is required, giving the effect of call-by-name. However, if a quoted parameter has free occurrences of Ids, when eval comes to be applied the current associations for those Ids may not be the correct ones. For this reason, the use of quote must be constrained; we will have more to say about this later in the chapter.

The reader may have wondered why we chose to give an informal description of FLISP semantics, rather than give a denotational description. There are two important considerations here. Firstly, denotational descriptions naturally specify call-by-name parameter passing, which corresponds to normal reduction in the λ-calculus. Secondly, the regime for association of names with values is also at variance with that which would be provided by default by a denotational description. It is possible to overcome both these problems within a denotational description, but it would introduce complications which would not help to clarify the matter at hand.

We should point out here that it is not necessary to use Defns at all, though it is quite convenient to be able to make some top level definitions. In fact, this facility as implemented in LISP systems introduces an inconsistency. This is the reason for the constraint noted in FLISP syntax with regard to Ids of Defn and Ids of Args; Ids of Defns and Ids of Args behave differently when evaluated as Atoms (see "the value of an Atom", above). They may also behave differently when they occur as the first Elem of a Brack to be evaluated. In some implementations, an Id of an Arg as first Elem of a Brack will cause execution to fail, even when the association for that Id is a Lambdaexp; under these circumstances, in order to achieve the effect of the invocation

```
(Id Elem₁ ... Elemₙ)
```

it will be necessary to write

```
(eval (list Id Elem₁ ... Elemₙ))
```

As an alternative to this clumsy expression, there may be a system-defined function, possibly called "apply", which may be used instead. Failing that, such a function could be defined, perhaps with the help of some non-standard features, enabling invocations such as that above to be written

```
(apply Id Elem₁ ... Elemₙ)
```

It is worth noting here that the reason why some LISP systems do not handle functions as parameters in a consistent way is probably that McCarthy's original concept of the language did not envisage this as a possibility; the language was essentially a first order language, even though it used notation derived from that of the λ-calculus. For the remainder of this chapter, we shall assume that the Ids of Defns and of Args behave in the same way as first Elem of a Brack, as described in the semantics above.

We have already seen that certain Atoms have very special significance in LISP, and so also in FLISP. In addition to the Special Forms already listed, in full LISP (or more precisely in LISP 1.5, as described in McCarthy et al. [McC]) there are several more Atoms with special meanings, which are in fact system-defined functions. Some of these are quite standard in any implementation, but others will be missing, or will be given different names, and there are usually many more added. Some quite standard ones we shall not use in FLISP, because they are not in the spirit of a functional programming language. The following is a list of those which are almost always available, with the stated meaning, and may be used in FLISP Programs:

System-defined functions: general utilities.

cons   two arguments, which must evaluate
to an Elem and a Brack respectively; delivers the Brack which consists of the elements of the given Brack, preceded by the Elem as first element.

car   one argument which must evaluate to a
Brack; delivers the first element of this Brack.

cdr   one argument which must evaluate to a
           Brack with at least one element; delivers the Brack
           obtained by removing the first element of that Brack.

list   indefinite number of arguments; delivers the
           Brack whose elements are the evaluated arguments in the
           same order.

eval   one argument; if the value of that argument is a
           Brack, then that Brack is in turn evaluated, and the
           result delivered, otherwise the value of the Atom which
           the argument produced is delivered.

mapcar   two arguments, the first of which must deliver a
           function description, or an Atom associated with a
           function description by a Defn, and the second of which
           must deliver a Brack; delivers the Brack obtained by
           applying the given function to the elements of that
           Brack in order.

atom   one argument; delivers t or nil, when the evaluated
           argument is or is not an Atom.

null   one argument; delivers t or nil, when the evaluated
           argument is or is not nil; also serves as
           logical negation.

eq   two arguments; delivers t or nil, when the evaluated
           arguments are or are not the same Elem.

numberp   one argument; delivers t or nil, when the evaluated
           argument is or is not a number.

and   indefinite number of arguments; delivers t if each
           evaluated argument delivers t, otherwise nil.

print   format of arguments varies, but allows printing on
           standard output channel; we shall use it mostly for
           error messages, since printing of Elems at Program level
           is implicit; delivers nil.

terpr   format of arguments varies; moves output to new line on
           standard output channel; delivers nil.

System-defined functions: arithmetic operations.

plus, times
           indefinite number of numeric arguments;
           they correspond to addition and multiplication.

diff   two numeric arguments; corresponds to subtraction.

minus   one numeric argument; changes the sign of its argument.

quotient two numeric arguments; for integer arguments performs integer division, otherwise performs real division.

lessp, greaterp
        two numeric arguments; deliver t or nil, according as to whether the first argument is or is not less than (greater than) the second argument.

minusp   one numeric argument; delivers t or nil, according as to whether the argument is or is not a negative number.

Note: here we have used "argument" to mean "evaluated argument".

Before we go any further, we are going to follow through the execution of a small Program, in order to come to understand the implications of the semantics. We trace the execution of the following Program:

```
(def inc (lambda (x) (plus x 1)))
(def treble (lambda (x) (times x 3)))
(treble (inc 5))
(exit)
```

using the notation that we employed in Chapter 2. The reader will recall that indentation is used to indicate inner computations, and that the arrow, <--, indicates a value being delivered, possibly being passed up more than one level:

```
associate (lambda (x) (plus x 1)) with inc
associate (lambda (x) (times x 3)) with treble
evaluate (treble (inc 5))
    invoke treble with (inc 5) as parameter
        evaluate (inc 5)
            invoke inc with 5 as parameter
                evaluate 5
                <-- 5
                associate 5 with x
                evaluate (plus x 1)
                    invoke plus with x and 1 as parameters
                        evaluate x
                        <-- 5
                        evaluate 1
                        <-- 1
        <------------- 6
```

```
associate 6 with x
evaluate (times x 3)
   invoke times with x and 3 as parameters
      evaluate x
      <-- 6
      evaluate 3
      <-- 3
<-------------- 18
```

EXERCISE

Execute by hand the following Program, using the tracing technique as above:

```
(def dub (lambda (x) (plus x x)))
(def dup (lambda (x) (list x x)))
(def infix
      (lambda (appl)
      (cond ((atom appl) appl)
            (t (eval (list (car (cdr appl))
                     (infix (car appl))
                     (infix (car (cdr (cdr appl)))))))
            )
      ))
)
(dub 12)
(dub (plus 3 4))
(mapcar (quote dub) (quote (3 5 7 9)))
(dup 1)
(dup (dup 2))
(infix (quote ((3 times 4) plus (5 times 6))))
(exit)
```

Make sure you understand exactly how the following six Elems come to be printed out:

    24, 14, (6 10 14 18), (1 1), ((2 2) (2 2)), 42.

7.2 AN EXAMPLE PROGRAM IN FLISP

As an example of how a Program in FLISP may be developed, we are going to write a Program which, given a function of one variable as a Lambdaexp, will compute the derivative of that function, again as a Lambdaexp, whose Body has been reasonably tidied up. For example, asked for the derivative of:

```
(lambda (x) (power (plus x 3) 2))
```

our Program will produce:

```
(lambda (x) (times 2 (plus x 3)))
```

We will use the design language to help us in the development of this Program.

```
define the function deriv which
        given function Fn as a Lambdaexp,
        produces a Lambdaexp with the same bound variable,
        and with Body obtained by finding the derivative of
        the Body of Fn with respect to that bound variable:-

(def deriv (lambda (Fn)
        when Fn is well formed
                produce the Brack consisting of
                        lambda,
                        the Args of Fn,
                        the derivative of the Body of Fn
                            wrt the bound variable of Fn,
        otherwise report ill formed
))
-----
when Fn is well formed ... otherwise report ill formed :-

(cond ((wellformed Fn)
                (list (quote lambda)
                      (args Fn)
                      (dwrt (boundvar Fn) (body Fn)))
        (t (print (quote illformed)))
))
-----
(args Fn) :- (car (cdr Fn))
-----
(boundvar Fn) :- (car (car (cdr Fn)))
-----
(body Fn) :- (car (cdr (cdr Fn)))
```

At this point, everything has been translated into FLISP, but of course the functions "wellformed" and "dwrt" need to be defined, thus giving rise to two new refinement problems. Note that we chose not to regard (args Fn) as a call to a function defined elsewhere, but instead we gave a replacement text for this; we treated (boundvar Fn) and (body Fn) in the same way.

Next we work on the first of the two new refinement problems:

```
define function wellformed,
        which, given an Elem,
              checks that it is a Brack,
              checks that its first Elem is lambda,
              checks that its second Elem is a Brack,
              checks that its third Elem is non-null,
              checks that the second Elem is a one Elem Brack,
                     that Elem an Id :-

(def wellformed (lambda (Elem)
        (cond    ((atom Elem) (print (quote (atomic function))))
                 ((null (eq (car Elem) (quote lambda)))
                                 (print (quote (no lambda))))
                 ((atom (second Elem))
                                 (print (quote (no varlist))))
                 ((null (third  Elem))
                                 (print (quote (no body))))
                 ((singlevar (second Elem)) t)
                 (t (print (quote (varlist too long)))))
        )
))

(def second (lambda (Elem)
        (cond    ((null (cdr Elem)) nil)
                 (t (car (cdr Elem)))
        )
))

(def third (lambda (Elem)
        (cond    ((null (cdr (cdr Elem))) nil)
                 (t (car (cdr (cdr Elem))))
        )
))

(def singlevar (lambda (Elem)
        (and (null (cdr Elem)) (null (numberp (car Elem)))))
))
```

The refinement of the definition of "wellformed" has become four Defns, three of which are really auxiliary to the Defn of wellformed. An important consideration here is the wish to keep any FLISP function definition to a manageable size, so that we can see how it works without the distraction of too much detail. Note also that the invocations of "print" within "wellformed" will deliver nil, besides having the side-effect of printing out their messages.

Next we turn our attention to the refinement of "dwrt"; here we decide to give Defns for functions "left" and "right" which are used several times in the Body of "dwrt", since their descriptions are of sufficient complexity that it would be undesirable to repeat them on every occasion. In the informal description of "dwrt" given here, we use the notation f′ to mean the derivative of f.

```
define function dwrt which
        given an Id, say Var, and an Elem, say Body
        simplifies the result of
                when Body is nil then "no function"
                when Body is a non-null Atom other than Var then 0,
                when Body is Var then 1,
                when Body is in effect f(Var) ** n
                        then n * f(Var) ** (n−1) * f′(Var),
                when Body is in effect f(Var) + g(Var)
                        then  f′(Var) + g′(Var),
                when Body is in effect f(Var) * g(Var)
                        then f(Var) * g′(Var) + f′(Var) * g(Var),
                otherwise "dont know" :-

(def dwrt
    (lambda (Var Body)
    (simplify
    (cond
        ((null Body) (quote nofunc))
        ((atom Body)
            (cond ((eq Var Body) 1) (t 0)))
        ((eq (majorop Body) (quote power))
          (list (quote times)
            (list (quote times) (right Body) (dwrt Var (left Body)))
            (list (quote power) (left Body) (diff (right Body) 1))
          ))
        ((eq (majorop Body) (quote plus))
            (list (quote plus)
                (dwrt Var (left Body)) (dwrt Var (right Body))
            ))
        ((eq (majorop Body) (quote times))
          (list (quote plus)
            (list (quote times) (left Body) (dwrt Var (right Body)))
            (list (quote times) (dwrt Var (left Body)) (right Body))
          ))
        (t (quote dontknow))
    )))
)
```

```
(def left (lambda (Body)
        (cond ((null (cdr Body)) nil)
              (t (car (cdr Body))))
        )
))

(def right (lambda (Body)
        (cond   ((null (left Body)) nil)
                ((null (cdr (cdr Body))) nil)
                (t (car (cdr (cdr Body)))))
        )
))
-----
(majorop Body) :- (car Body)
```

Again, a new refinement problem has been created, that of defining a function "simplify", which given an expression in the usual FLISP prefix form, performs some simplification where possible.

```
define function simplify, which given a Brack, say Form,
        when Form is an Atom, returns that Atom unchanged;
        otherwise, having simplified the left and right operands,
            giving Elems Lform and Rform say,
            when both Lform and Rform are numbers,
                returns the result of applying the major op,
            when Rform is 0, and major op is power, returns 1,
            when Rform is 1, and major op is power, returns Lform,
            when major op is plus and one operand is 0,
                returns other operand,
            when major op is times and one operand is 0, returns 0,
            when major op is times and one operand is 1,
                returns other operand,
            otherwise returns the Brack with Elems the major op,
                Lform and Rform :-

(def simplify
    (lambda (Form)
    (cond
        ((atom Form) Form)
        (t  ((lambda (Lform Rform)
                (cond
                    ((and (numberp Lform) (numberp Rform))
                        (eval (list (majorop Form) Lform Rform)))
                    ((eq (majorop Form) (quote power))
                        (cond
                            ((eq Rform 0) 1)
                            ((eq Rform 1) Lform)
                            (t (list (quote power) Lform Rform))
                        ))
```

```
                    ((eq (majorop Form) (quote plus))
                        (cond
                            ((eq Lform 0) Rform)
                            ((eq Rform 0) Lform)
                            (t (list (quote plus) Lform Rform))
                        ))
                    ((eq (majorop Form) (quote times))
                        (cond
                            ((eq Lform 0) 0)
                            ((eq Rform 0) 0)
                            ((eq Lform 1) Rform)
                            ((eq Rform 1) Lform)
                            (t (list (quote times) Lform Rform))
                        ))
                    (t (list (majorop Form) Lform Rform))
                )
            )
            (simplify (left Form)) (simplify (right Form))
        )
    )
  ))
)
```

Note that we use an inner Lambdaexp, which has the effect that simplification of the left and right operands happens only once; this device can be used to provide, in simple cases, an auxiliary definition mechanism, like that of SUGAR. Also note that the functions "left" and "right" which were defined as auxiliary function definitions for "dwrt" are again needed here.

We are almost finished now; it only remains to define the function "power" which is referred to by "simplify" and may not be defined by the system available. We also give some illustrative examples of the use of the "deriv" function we have now defined.

```
define the function power, which given parameters x and p,
        checks that both x and p are numeric,
        checks that p is positive,
        when p is 0 gives 1,
        when p is 1 gives x,
        otherwise, gives product of x and x to power (p−1)
        :-

(def power
    (lambda (x p)
        (cond ((null (numberp x)) nil)
              ((null (numberp p)) nil)
              ((lessp p 0) nil)
              ((eq p 0) 1)
              ((eq p 1) x)
```

```
                    (t (times x (power x (diff p 1)))))
          )
  ))

  ---
  examples of use of deriv function defined above :-

  (deriv (quote (lambda (x) (plus (power x 3) (times 4 x)))))

  (deriv (quote (lambda (y) (times (plus y 3) (plus y 2)))))

  (mapcar (deriv
            (quote (lambda (u)
                    (plus (power u 3) (times 3 (power u 2)))))
            (list 1 2 3 4 5 6))

  (deriv (deriv (quote (lambda (x) (power x 4)))))
```

An interesting feature of this Program is that it illustrates one of the important properties of LISP, which is that data and program are indistinguishable. In LISP we can take apart the Lambdaexp which represents a function, and we can construct the derivative function from component parts. In SUGAR neither of these is possible, unless we treat the given function as a quoted character string, and produce a derivative function which is again a character string; this would involve us in a level of syntax analysis which is quite unnecessary in LISP, and even then we still cannot use the derivative function produced, unless there is a conversion operator from character string to function description. However, it should be pointed out that unconstrained use of this feature of LISP is certainly not in the spirit of functional programming. The point is that a functional program should produce the same results if any of the function definitions within it is replaced by a definition which though differently constructed from primitives and other defined functions is equivalent in the sense that it realizes the same mathematical function.

EXERCISES

1. Write a Defn in FLISP for the function "leastproperdivisor" which can be described as follows:

```
function leastproperdivisor, given two integer parameters,
        say n and s, where  2 ≤ s ≤ n,
        finds the smallest  integer, say d,
        such that s ≤ d ≤ n, and d divides n exactly.
```

Now write a Defn for the following function, using your Defn of leastproperdivisor as an auxiliary function:

```
function primefacs, given an integer n, n ≥ 2,
        produces a Brack representing the prime factorization
        of n, the factors presented in ascending order.
```

In the first instance, write simple versions, without worrying about efficiency, but then try to increase efficiency by improving the method or by the use of auxiliary definitions which reduce the need for recomputation of intermediate values.

2. Write a Defn in FLISP for the function "deliver", which behaves in the following way:

the effect of a call such as

```
(deliver (quote Elem₀)
  where (quote ((Id₁ Elem₁) (Id₂ Elem₂) ... (Idₙ Elemₙ)))
  )
```

should be to evaluate $Elem_0$, where the value of any free occurrence of any Id_p, where $1 \leq p \leq n$, is to be taken as the value of $Elem_p$.

Assume that the auxiliary definitions of Id_1 ... Id_n are not recursive or mutually recursive, that is, none of the $Elem_1$ ... $Elem_n$ refer to any of Id_1 ... Id_n. The second parameter to the function deliver is a dummy, which simply absorbs a separator such as "where".

3. Modify the Body of "dwrt", defined in this section, to handle "plus" and "times" with an indefinite number of arguments, and modify the Body of "simplify" accordingly.

4. Write a Defn for a function "collect" which, given a function Body whose form is equivalent to a polynomial in a single variable, will multiply out factors, collect terms, and reorder powers of the variable into descending order. For example, given:

```
(times (plus x 1) (plus (times 2 x) 3))
```

the function should produce:

```
(plus (times 2 (power x 2)) (times 5 x) 3)
```

5. Write a Defn of "mapcar" as described in the earlier list of functions generally available.

6. Write a Defn for a function "tabulate", described as follows:

```
the function tabulate,
        given a function, say F, taking one integer parameter,
        and two integers, say low and upp, low ≤ upp,
prints out the values of F(low), F(low+1), ... F(upp).
```

7.3 USING THE SPECIAL FORM quote

The special form quote is an essential part of LISP, and indeed of FLISP, because it provides the mechanism by which the form of a non-atomic argument can be specified, without the usual function invocation mechanism being called into action. It can also be used to quote an atomic argument, so that we can refer to an Atom itself rather than to its associated value. However, it allows us to do something which is very undesirable within a functional programming language: it allows us to carry an Atom from an environment in which there is a well-defined meaning for that Atom into another environment in which there is a quite different meaning for that same Atom. Now it would be rather difficult for the implementor of the language to recognize when this is being done, and it would also slow down the evaluation mechanism in the innocent cases of the use of quote. As a result, many implementations of LISP have made the assumption that in order to determine the association with any Atom at any point during evaluation, the most recent association is taken, which means that the Atom can be trapped by an association established in order to perform an inner evaluation. This is also the effect of the FLISP semantics as defined earlier. What is so unsatisfactory about this is that the meaning of a Program could be changed by using different Ids in the Args of one of the functions defined in that Program; in particular, identical function invocations could produce different values, because for some Atoms the associations were different in the environments in which those invocations were carried out.

The problem arises when quote is applied to an Elem in which there are free occurrences of Ids. For example in:

```
(quote (lambda (x) (plus x y)))
```

the Id y is free, and must take its meaning from the surrounding context. On the other hand, x is not free, because it is the Id of the Args of the Lambdaexp, and does not depend on the surrounding context for its meaning. The system-defined Atoms lambda and plus mean the same in any context, so the question does not arise for them. Now consider the following Program:

```
//powersums program

    (def sigma (lambda (fn low upp)
          (cond ((greaterp low upp) 0)
                (t (plus (fn low) (sigma fn (plus low 1) upp))))))

    (def powersum (lambda (n low upp)
          (sigma (quote (lambda (x) (power x n))) low upp)))

    (powersum 4 1 6)
    (exit)
```

Assume "power" is defined as before, in the derivatives program. The free n in the argument of quote will be given the value 4, associated with the n of the Args of "powersum", using the association rule defined in FLISP semantics, so that the sum of the fourth powers of the integers 1 to 6 will be computed as required; but what would happen if sigma were defined as follows?

```
    (def sigma (lambda (fn m n)
          (cond ((greaterp m n) 0)
                (t (plus (fn m) (sigma fn (plus m 1) n))))))
```

The sixth powers, not the fourth powers, would be summed. Changing the names of the variables of sigma has changed the meaning of the Program. Of course, what we really wanted to say is that the argument to be passed to sigma should be

```
    (lambda (x) (power x n))
    where n has the value of the argument passed to powersum
```

How shall we modify FLISP to remedy this unsatisfactory state of affairs? There seem to be three things we could do:

we could adopt a different rule for determining what is the correct association for an Atom;

we could insist that quote must deliver not only its argument, but also an environment which determines what are the associations for any free Atoms occurring in that argument;

we could restrict the use of quote, so that the existing association rule is adequate.

The first approach is theoretically possible; presumably we would want the associations with Atoms which are wrapped up by quote to be carried along, so that when they are eventually unwrapped those associations have not changed. This amounts to determining the association of an Atom by its position in the text of the Program, rather than dynamically according to the rule given in FLISP semantics; this is familiar to us not only from SUGAR but also from block structured imperative languages such as ALGOL-68 and PASCAL. These imperative languages were designed with a certain implementation method in mind; that method is not easily extended to deal with the full implications of the ability to create new function descriptions at run time. For this reason LISP implementations have generally not adopted this approach, and so we are not free to do so in FLISP either. In ALGOL-like languages, it is either forbidden to deliver a function whose body contains references to the local variables of the function which delivers it, or if it is not expressly forbidden, then to do this would have unpredictable results. This is because when the values of those variables are eventually needed, they may no longer exist according to the rules which define the lifetimes of variables.

As an example, the following function definition:

```
define function partadd, which given parameter m,
     produces the function which given parameter n,
            produces the value of m + n
```

is illegal if literally translated into ALGOL-68, because the body of the function (or actually it would be a PROC) makes reference to the local parameter name of partadd. PASCAL avoids the problem by not allowing functions to deliver functions.

Considering the second of the approaches suggested above, in LISP 1.5 there is a system-defined Atom "function" which is to be used instead of quote for an argument which has Atoms in it whose associations must be preserved. (Note that some implementations define "function", but it may not do what has just been described; instead, it may be used as a means to access the function description associated with an Atom by a Defn.) This leaves the implementor free to assume that the programmer does not mind what might happen to an Atom occurring in the argument of a quote, but provides a mechanism for those occasions when it is necessary to carry through the environment.

Since we cannot assume that the LISP system which is available to us has a correct implementation of "function", in FLISP we adopt the third approach, that is, we restrict the use of quote.

Quote Constraint

> quote may not be used in any way which allows a Lambdaexp which has free occurrences of Ids to be applied in an environment which could override the correct associations for those free Ids

In the powersums program, it certainly violates our constraint to write:

```
(quote (lambda (x) (power x n)))
```

as the argument to be passed to sigma, as we have seen. Clearly we shall have to be very careful when an argument of quote has free occurrences of Ids of Args. On the other hand, we could write

```
(list (quote lambda) (list (quote x))
      (list (quote power) (quote x) n ))
```

as the argument to sigma; in this latter form, the occurrence of n will be evaluated in the current environment before being incorporated into the Lambdaexp which is being constructed, and although x is quoted, this is quite safe because x is going to be the Id of the Args of that Lambdaexp. We could always achieve the effect we want by using the function "list" in this way, building a Lambdaexp from its Atomic components, but this would produce unnecessarily obscure Programs. In the next section, we are going to define a function "closure" which will allow us to write something much more natural in place of unwieldy expressions of this kind.

It is worth noting that some LISP programmers quite deliberately use quote in the way we have said is dangerous (perhaps because its effect is very much like the call-by-name parameter mechanism in ALGOL-60); we would not recommend this, since in any case there is usually a better way to achieve the desired effect without violating the principles of functional programming.

EXERCISE

The function "deriv" defined earlier takes a function as a parameter and delivers a function as a result; why is there no violation of the Quote Constraint in this case?

7.4 CLOSURE

Throughout this book, when we define a function, or a group of functions, this is usually done in order to solve some specific problem. Functions may also be defined which would be useful as ancillary functions in a wide variety of applications, which gives the effect of extending the language. The ability of LISP to analyze the structure of its function specifications makes it particularly powerful in this respect, and the special functions which we are going to define in this section are examples of this.

Before we define "closure", we need a simpler function called "assoc", which satisfies the following informal description:

```
define the function assoc which
    given two arguments
        the first a Brack, say AssInvoc,
            representing a function invocation,
        the second a Brack, say AssIds,
            which consists of a list of Ids
            whose current associations must be used to ensure
            correct evaluation of that invocation in some
            other environment;
    produces a Brack,
        whose first Elem is a Lambdaexp,
        whose Args is AssIds,
        whose Body is AssInvoc,
        whose remaining Elems are the current associations
            for the Ids of AssIds in corresponding order
```

As an example of the effect of "assoc", the invocation:

```
(assoc (quote (power x n)) (quote (n)))
```

when evaluated in an environment in which n has associated value 4 will produce:

```
((lambda (n) (power x n)) (quote 4))
```

Note that the current value of n, 4 in this case, is quoted; in this simple example this is unnecessary but harmless, but associated values may also be Lambdaexps or Bracks, and then we must shield them from further evaluation when they are eventually used as arguments.

The reader may wonder why "assoc" produces a Brack which represents the application of a Lambdaexp to a list of arguments, when it might simply substitute the associated values which must be preserved, giving for the present example the simpler form:

```
(power x 4)
```

The most important reason for this is that some of the associated values may be recursively defined; to substitute such a value would produce a form which still contained a reference to the Id concerned, which would not give the effect we want. As we have defined "assoc", the effect is that when the resulting invocation comes to be evaluated, an inner environment is constructed which preserves any inter-relationships between the associated values of the list of Ids. Note that it may be necessary to include in the second argument of "assoc" Ids which do not occur in the first argument, but which occur in the current association for an Id which does occur in that argument. If the quote constraint were not adhered to it could become very difficult to know the complete set of Ids which were necessary. However, the constraint implies that arguments to functions will not have free occurrences of Ids; thus when a function, say F, must deliver another function whose correct evaluation depends on preserving certain associations, we never need to consider any Ids other than those included in the Args of F, or in the Args of a lexically surrounding Lambdaexp.

Following closely the above description, here is the FLISP Defn for "assoc":

```
(def assoc (lambda (AssInvoc AssIds)
        (cons (list (quote lambda) AssIds AssInvoc)
            (mapcar
                (quote (lambda (AssId)
                            (list (quote quote) (eval AssId))))
                AssIds
            )
        )
 ))
```

Now we can describe the "closure" function as follows:

```
define closure as the function which
      given two arguments
            the first a Lambdaexp, say CloFun,
            the second a Brack, say CloIds,
                  which consists of a list of the Ids whose
                  associations are needed for correct evaluation of
                  the Body of CloFun
      produces a function with the same Args as the given function,
            whose Body consists of the result of applying assoc
            to the Body of CloFun and the list of Ids
```

The function "closure" is designed to ensure that it is always safe to give a quoted Lambdaexp as its first argument, so long as the second argument consists of a list of all those Ids whose current associations are needed to ensure correct evaluation when that Lambdaexp is applied. As a simple example, if we replace the Defn of "powersum" in the powersums program by

```
(def powersum (lambda (n low upp)
      (sigma
            (closure
                  (quote (lambda (x) (power x n)))
                  (quote (n))
            )
            low upp
      )
))
```

then the Lambdaexp which is passed to sigma will be:

```
(lambda (x)
         ((lambda (n) (power x n)) (quote 4)))
```

when "powersum" is invoked for arguments 4, 1, 6. Here n is no longer free, and will always receive the value 4 when a value for x is supplied. It is now quite simple to write a Defn for "closure" as follows:

```
(def closure (lambda (CloFun CloIds)
         (list (quote lambda) (car (cdr CloFun))
               (assoc (car (cdr (cdr CloFun))) CloIds)
         )
))
```

We will think of "assoc" and "closure" as FLISP system-defined functions; we must regard the names AssForm, AssId, AssIds, CloFun and CloIds as ineligible for use as the Ids of Args of other functions.

We conclude this section, and the chapter, with a set of exercises which give some practice in defining higher order functions in FLISP, and also show one way in which potentially infinite data structures could be handled. Although we feel that working on these exercises will help the reader to understand more about the nature of functional programming, we certainly do not wish to imply that we feel that FLISP is a suitable language for functional programming on an everyday basis. Quite apart from the fact that FLISP is a sublanguage of LISP, which contains many features alien to the functional style, we feel that the syntax of the language, and especially the multitude of brackets which this entails, are quite unsuitable for the production of reliable and intelligible programs. It is our view that LISP and variants of it are completely superseded by the newer functional languages which have come into existence in recent years. No doubt LISP will live on for many years since the artificial intelligence community has a considerable investment in its continued availability.

EXERCISE

1. Using the most recent definition of "powersum", and the earlier definition of sigma, trace the evaluation of the invocation

    (powersum 4 2 3)

in the style of Section 7.1.

2. Why is it necessary to restrict the use of the Ids used as Args of "closure" and "assoc"?

3. Write a Defn in FLISP for the function firstdiffs, corresponding to the following SUGAR definition:

    firstdiffs is [series] ([x] series(x + 1) − series(x))

where the parameter is expected to be a function from integers to integers. Now, using the function firstdiffs, define the more general function diffs, described informally as follows:

```
the function diffs,
        given a function, say F, from integers to integers,
        and a positive integer, say n,
produces the function corresponding to the nth differences of F,
```

```
that is, when n = 1 it produces firstdiffs(F),
          when n > 1 it produces firstdiffs( diffs(F, n-1) )
```

Use the function tabulate (see Exercise 6 of Section 7.2) when testing your Defns of firstdiffs and diffs.

4. If we want to be able to handle potentially infinite lists in FLISP, we can do this with the help of a set of auxiliary Defns which allow us to suspend and unsuspend Elems. For example, if we make the following definition:

```
(def suspend (lambda (SuForm SuIds)
          (list (quote Su) (assoc SuForm SuIds))
))
```

where "assoc" is the function defined earlier in this section, then consider the Defn:

```
(def from (lambda (n)
          (list n (suspend (quote (from (plus n 1))) (quote (n))))
)).
```

The result of evaluating (from 1) will be:

```
(1 (Su ((lambda (n) (from (plus n 1))) (quote 1)))),
```

which represents the infinite list (1 2 3 4 5 ...)

Write Defns for the following functions, assuming that suspended Elems may be encountered, flagged by "Su" as above:

```
the function head, given a potentially infinite list,
          produces the first Elem of that list;

the function tail, given a potentially infinite list,
          produces the potentially infinite list obtained by
          removing the first Elem;

the function show, given a potentially infinite list,
          prints the Elems of that list, until some
          system violation occurs, such as arithmetic
          overflow, stack space exhausted, etc.
```

(Note: You may find that your Defn for show allows rather few elements to be printed out before exhausting the space which your implementation reserves for information about parameters during function invocation. The function show is tail recursive, which means that it is never necessary to return from nested recursive calls, and in such cases, by using the flow-of-control features of full LISP, an iterative version of show can be written. Such an iterative version is given in Appendix 2.)

5. Write a Defn for the function star, described as follows:

```
the function star,
        given an initial value, say init,
        and a suitable one-place function, say F,
produces the infinite list
        (init, F(init), F(F(init)), F(F(F(init))), ... )
```

Now consider the function nextrow, described as follows:

```
the function nextrow,
        given a Brack, say row, of length n,
produces a Brack, of length n+1,
        whose first Elem is the first Elem of row,
        whose last Elem is the last Elem of row,
        whose pth Elem, for 2 ≤ p ≤ n,
            is the sum of the (p—1)th and pth Elems of row
```

Use star and nextrow to produce the potentially infinite Pascal triangle of binomial coefficients, and use show, perhaps slightly modified to print successive elements on separate lines, to print it out as far as possible.

6. (A more difficult exercise.) Produce a set of rules which allows translation from SUGAR into FLISP. One of the more tricky rules is that for the translation of auxiliary definitions, when mutual recursion is allowed. Try out your rules on some of your SUGAR programs. (Note: we have included a set of translation rules in Appendix 3.)

BIBLIOGRAPHY

McCarthy et al. is the definitive document for LISP 1.5. King and Hayes give a very readable introduction to LISP, with plenty of self-test examples, whereas Sussman is an advanced and thorough treatment of programming in LISP, and of implementation issues, from the standpoint of functional programming. Henderson, as mentioned earlier, is a more advanced and comprehensive treatment of much of the ground covered in the present text.

[Dar] Darlington J., Henderson P. and Turner D.A. "Functional Programming and its Applications", Cambridge University Press, 1982.

[Hen] Henderson P. "Functional Programming: Application and Implementation", Prentice-Hall International, 1980.

[Kin] King M. and Hayes P. "Programming in LISP", in "Computational Semantics" (edited by Charniak E. and Wilks Y.), North-Holland, 1976.

[McC] McCarthy J., Abrahams P.W., Edwards D.J., Hart T.P. and Levin M.I. "LISP 1.5 Programmer's Manual", MIT Press, 1962.

[Sus] Sussman G.J. "LISP, Programming and Implementation", in [Dar].

8

OTHER FUNCTIONAL LANGUAGES

In our discussion of SUGAR and LISP, we have avoided many complex issues. This is not surprising because SUGAR was designed as a pedagogical tool and was intended as a vehicle for teaching the main principles of functional programming. As such its syntax and semantics are small and elegant. SUGAR has been applied to the solution of a large and diverse set of problems; however, more complex languages often allow more elegant solutions. In this chapter we identify some further facilities that are provided by other functional languages and look at three particular languages, KRC, HOPE and FP, all of which have features that raise their expressive power above that of SUGAR. Rather than give exhaustive descriptions of each of these languages, we shall focus on the distinctive features of each. We finish the chapter with a brief discussion of some of the issues that are still being investigated by research workers.

8.1 ADDITIONAL FACILITIES

The issues that we wish to consider can be categorized under five headings. We show below which issues are addressed by which languages:

1. Pattern-matching of parameters
   KRC and HOPE
2. Complex data structuring operators
   KRC and HOPE

177

3. Typing of objects
      HOPE
4. Programmer-defined data types
      HOPE and FP
5. Complex function-forming operators
      FP

We briefly look at each of these issues and justify their inclusion in functional programming languages.

8.1.1 Pattern-matching

In both KRC and HOPE functions are defined by a series of equations. Each equation specifies what the function is to do with parameters of a particular structure. The execution mechanism must be given the "intelligence" to match actual parameters with the patterns used in the definition of a function so that it can decide which equation to use. This facility, which offers an alternative to conditional expressions, often leads to clearer and more concise definitions.

8.1.2 Complex Data Structures

The requirement of simplicity in the design of SUGAR has meant that the only form of data structure in SUGAR is the list structure. There are many applications in which richer data structures are essential for good programs. KRC addresses this problem to some extent by allowing the programmer to represent sets of values (in the mathematical sense), although these are represented as lists. On the other hand, HOPE provides an altogether richer set of types and type constructors that are built into the language and, as we shall see later, the programmer can also define new types.

8.1.3 Typing

Most modern imperative programming languages require the programmer to specify the type of every non-literal object that is used in a program. The advantage of this approach is that extensive compile-time checking can be performed to prevent type errors occurring at run-time. This is an important issue because type errors are often symptomatic of underlying logical errors which may not be easy to trace from run-time error messages. In contrast, SUGAR is a type free language. There are advantages to the latter approach, one of which is that functions can be defined for which the type of any particular parameter is one of a range of types. These are called polymorphic functions; in a strongly typed imperative language, a new definition would be required for every conceivable set of parameter types. HOPE strikes a compromise between these two extremes. It is a strongly typed language, but it allows polymorphic functions and the type information provided by the programmer is kept to a reasonable minimum.

8.1.4 Programmer-defined Data Types

One of the most powerful techniques of the structured programming school is the use of data abstractions or abstract data types. An abstract data type is a programmer-defined type that has been tailored to the solution of a particular problem. The idea is that objects of an abstract type can only be constructed and accessed using a set of constructor and observer functions that are defined at the same time as the type. The implementation of the type is completely hidden from the user. Both HOPE and an extended version of FP allow the definition of data abstractions. Because much of the work on FP is still experimental and because the language is so radically different from any of the others, we only concentrate on data abstractions in the HOPE section. This facility is also included in imperative languages; data abstractions were first introduced via the CLASS concept in SIMULA and are to be found in more recent languages such as ADA.

8.1.5 Complex Function-forming Operators

Finally, apart from FP, all of the languages basically use one function-forming operation, that of functional abstraction. The drawback of this is that the programmer is often encouraged, or even forced, to overspecify a solution to a problem. For example, the programmer might use tail recursion to process the elements of a list which is a level of detail that may be totally unnecessary to the solution of the problem. FP has a set of high level function-forming operators which allay this problem to a certain extent.

8.2 KRC

The starting point for the language KRC, developed by David Turner, is the representation of function definitions as sets of equations, as it was for his earlier language SASL. For example, a KRC definition of the Fibonacci function might be:

```
fib 1 = 1
fib 2 = 1
fib n = fib(n-1) + fib(n-2)
```

or it could also be

```
fib n = 1, n = 1
      = 1, n = 2
      = fib(n-1) + fib(n-2), n > 2
```

These two definitions illustrate the fact that we can indicate different cases of a function definition either by using conditions on the right hand side, or by specifying patterns on the left hand side which must match a particular argument in order that the equation may be used for that argument. When using patterns on the left hand side, the equations must be given in an order such that more specific patterns occur before less specific patterns. Note that it is not necessary to bracket arguments, except where some ambiguity could arise. As another example of a function definition using patterns to be matched, we give a definition of a function "total", which adds up the elements of a list of integers:

```
total [ ] = 0
total (a : x) = a + total x
```

The empty list is represented by "[ ]", and the notation "a : x" is a pattern which will match any non-empty list, and will allow us to refer to the head of the list as "a", and the tail of the list as "x" on the right hand side. When we come to look at HOPE, we will see that this idea of pattern-matching for structured arguments can be extended to any domain whose elements are characterized by particular constructor functions. In KRC the only primitive constructor function is ":", which corresponds to "cons" in LISP or the prefix operator ":" in SUGAR.

Besides the pattern-matching facility, which allows functions involving list arguments to be specified very neatly, the other important feature is the ability to compute with sets of objects. A set of objects is represented in KRC by a list, and there are abbreviations for certain sets, such as [1..10] which represents the set [1,2,3,4,5,6,7,8,9,10], and [2..] which represents the set of positive integers greater than 1. There is also a notation for set abstraction, as examples:

```
{ x*x | x <- [1..100]}  is the set {1,4,9,16,25,...,...,10000}

{ [x,y] | x, y <- [1..3]; x > y }
                   is the set {[2,1], [3,1], [3,2]}
```

In each case, the vertical bar means "such that", which corresponds to the usual mathematical notation, and semi-colons may be read as "and"; the left arrow is used to indicate the set over which the variable (or variables) on its left may range, and is presumably meant to look like the usual membership symbol of mathematics. Thus we could define:

```
cartesianproduct x y = { [a,b] | a <- x; b <- y}

permutations [ ] = [ [ ] ]
permutations x = { a:p | a <- x; p <- permutations(x -- [a]) }
```

where the operator "--" represents set difference.

The pattern-matching and set abstraction features allow for very concise specifications; for example, the primes may be generated, by sieving (see Chapter 2) as follows:

```
primes = sieve [2..]
sieve (p : x) = p : sieve {n | n <- x; \ (n % p = 0)}
```

where "%" is the remainder operator, and "\" is the system-defined negation operator.

We end this brief introduction to KRC with a more significant example, which demonstrates the economy of expression which can be achieved by use of set abstraction. We will look at the problem of coloring a map using four different colors under the constraint that no two countries which have any common border may be the same color.

We will have to provide information about which countries are neighbors, and this will be done by supplying a list of pairs of countries which border on each other. For example, we might define "borders" as follows:

```
borders = [ ["France","Spain"], ["France","Germany"],
            ["France","Switzerland"], ["France","Belgium"],
            ["France","Luxembourg"], ["France","Italy"],
```

```
["Spain","Portugal"], ["Germany","Austria"], ..., ...]
```

and suppose we define the available colors as follows:-

```
colorset = ["red","green","yellow","orange"]
```

Now we define a function "coloring":-

```
define function coloring, which
          given a list of (distinct) countries,
          assuming that "borders" can be consulted to
               discover which countries border on each other,
               and that "colorset" defines colors available,
          produces the set of all possible colorings,
               satisfying the constraint that no two countries
               which border each other may be the same color
          :-
coloring [ ] = [ [ ] ]
coloring (country : othercountries)
          = { [ [newcolor, country] ] ++ subcoloring |
               newcolor <- colorset;
               subcoloring <- coloring othercountries;
               noconflicts subcoloring [newcolor, country]}
```

which says that the empty set is the only coloring of an empty set of countries, and that the colorings of a list of countries consist of colorings of the tail of that list, extended by a color for the head of the list, which does not violate the constraint. (Note: $++$ is the concatenation operator for lists.) Next we need to define a function "noconflicts" which will test that the constraint is satisfied:

```
define function noconflicts, which
          given a list "subcoloring" of [color, country] pairs,
               and a pair [newcolor, newcountry],
          will check that the pair [newcolor, newcountry]
               does not cause violation of the constraint
               when appended to the list subcoloring,
               assuming that subcoloring is itself consistent
          :-
noconflicts subcoloring [newcolor, newcountry]
          = and { noconflict colcon [newcolor, newcountry] |
               colcon <- subcoloring }
```

which says that there will be no conflict between the new [color,country] pair and the given list of pairs if there is no conflict with any member of that list. Thus we need now to define "noconflict":

```
define function noconflict, which
        given pairs [oldcolor, oldcountry] and [newcolor, newcountry]
        will check that no violation of the constraint arises
                as a result of the two color,country pairings
                involved here
        :-
noconflict [oldcolor, oldcountry] [newcolor, newcountry]
    = or [ \ (newcolor = oldcolor),
            and [ \ ( member borders [newcountry, oldcountry] ),
                    \ ( member borders [oldcountry, newcountry] ) ] ]
```

which says that either the two colors involved are different, or the two countries do not have a common border. (Note: "and", "or" and "member" are system-defined.)

Now if we wanted only a single possible coloring, we could ask for this by writing:

```
hd(coloring ["France","Spain","Germany", ..., ...]) ?
```

Finally, we gather together all the functions defined for this example:

```
borders = [ ["France","Spain"], ["France","Germany"],
            ["France","Switzerland"], ["France","Belgium"],
            ["France","Luxembourg"], ["France","Italy"],
            ["Spain","Portugal"], ["Germany","Austria"], ..., ...]

colorset = ["red","green","yellow","orange"]

coloring [ ] = [ [ ] ]
coloring (country : othercountries)
    = { [ [newcolor, country] ] ++ subcoloring |
            newcolor <− colorset;
            subcoloring <− coloring othercountries;
            noconflicts subcoloring [newcolor, country]}

noconflicts subcoloring [newcolor, newcountry]
    = and { noconflict colcon [newcolor, newcountry] |
            colcon <− subcoloring }

noconflict [oldcolor, oldcountry] [newcolor, newcountry]
    = or [ \ (newcolor = oldcolor),
            and [ \ ( member borders [newcountry, oldcountry] ),
                    \ ( member borders [oldcountry, newcountry] ) ] ]
```

We can see here the terseness of expression that the language allows for this kind of problem, which would traditionally have required the programmer to specify in detail the backtracking mechanism. In the above KRC program, by making use of the set abstraction facility, all the detail of the organization of the backtracking has been left to the implementation, leaving the programmer free to specify the solution to the programming problem at a more convenient level of abstraction. The pattern-matching facility is also a very powerful means of expression, since at the same time as recognizing a particular structure of arguments of a function, it also provides names for the components of that structure.

On the other hand, the lack of a local definition mechanism like the "where" construct in SUGAR, could prove quite inconvenient; one may be forced to make extra definitions of functions available globally, when this may not be desirable, or one may be forced to confuse levels of detail within a function definition. However it should be noted that one of the issues which interested David Turner when he designed KRC was whether a local definition facility was a desirable feature of a functional language; it seems that his experience with KRC has convinced him that it is.

EXERCISES

1. Translate the engint program of Chapter 2 into KRC.

2. There is a children's game in which the players stand in a ring, and a counting down process is repeated, each time eliminating one of the players who then leaves the ring, until only one player remains, who is the winner or "survivor". Before the game starts, one child is selected as the starting point for the counting down process, and a number is chosen which will be used for the counting each time. Beginning at the starting point, the children count down going left around the ring, and the child reached on the count of one is the one to leave the ring. Counting down is begun again at the next child to the left of the one who has just left the ring.

Write a KRC program which, given the number of children in the ring initially and the number to be used for the counting, determines who will be the survivor.

3. Suppose we are given information about the distances between pairs of cities, the information being given as a set of triples (C1, C2, DI), the significance of such a triple being that there is a road of distance DI between cities C1 and C2, not passing through any of the other cities. Assume that for any pair of cities C1 and C2 there is at most

one such triple. Now suppose we want to be able to work out the shortest route between any two given cities.

We define a path as a sequence of cities, where every pair of successive elements of the sequence corresponds to one of the given triples, in that the two cities concerned are the two cities which form the first and second elements of that triple. A path whose first element is some city C, is called a path from C. A path from C whose last element is some other city D, is called a path from C to D. The length of a path is one less than the number of cities on the path; the distance of a path is the sum of the distances for all the triples corresponding to the successive pairs on the path.

Now consider the sequence P_1, P_2, P_3, ..., of sets of paths from C, where P_i is the set of all paths from C of length at most i. Within P_i there could be several paths from C to the same city, say E, each of these paths representing different ways of going from C to E. Now consider the sequence Q_1, Q_2, Q_3, ..., of sets of paths from C, where each Q_i is a subset of P_i, where each element of Q_i, being a path from C to E say, is an element of P_i amongst all paths from C to E in P_i, with the lowest distance. If we generate the sequence of sets Q_1, Q_2, Q_3, ..., in order, at some stage we will find that two successive elements of the sequence are identical, because it is not possible that any of the elements of any Q_i can contain a path with loops in it. At this stage, the shortest path from C to any city D can be found by searching the Q_i last computed.

Write a KRC program embodying these ideas.

8.3 HOPE

The major new issues raised by HOPE, a language designed by Burstall and his co-workers at Edinburgh University, are strong typing and the introduction of data abstractions. As we noted in the introduction, HOPE also uses equations and pattern-matching in function definitions. We will introduce the notation by example in the context of our discussion of the typing and data abstraction facilities of HOPE.

8.3.1 Types

Although HOPE is a typed language, the compiler uses context as much as possible to assign the correct type to an object. The compiler is able to do this because HOPE is a functional language and thus every name is assigned a single value within any given context. Instead of having to define the type of every non-literal object, the only objects that have to be declared in a HOPE program are functions. A familiar example, the factorial function, is illustrated below:

```
dec fac : num —> num;
--- fac(n) <= n * fac(n—1);
--- fac(0) <= 1;
```

The "dec" statement declares "fac" to be a function that has a single parameter of type "num" (the natural numbers and zero) and produces a result of type "num". Notice that in HOPE, unlike KRC, the less specific cases must be specified first. Each clause of the definition of a function is introduced by "---" at the beginning of the line and the semi-colon is an optional terminator that we shall usually omit. HOPE has a number of built-in types, one of which is "num"; some of the others are shown below:

```
truval        -        truth values
char          -        characters
list          -        lists of values
set           -        sets of values
```

The "list" and "set" types are to be used in conjunction with other types; for example, the declaration of a sort function might be:

```
dec sort : list num —> list num
```

One of the disadvantages of strongly typed conventional languages such as PASCAL is the difficulty of defining "polymorphic" functions. A polymorphic function is a function that defines a transformation which is applicable to a range of different parameter types. For example, the SUGAR function shown below, given a boolean "a", will work for any types of parameters "b" and "c":

```
poly is [a,b,c] if a then b else c endf;
```

In PASCAL the programmer would need to declare a separate function for each set of parameter types that "poly" is to be used with. Even in this way, PASCAL does not capture the full semantics of the SUGAR definition, because a PASCAL function can only return values which have a simple type. Also "b" and "c" would both have to be of the same type. The fact that one could use procedures and variant records to alleviate some of these problems does not really compensate for PASCAL's shortcomings in this area.

The ability to define polymorphic functions is an important notational device that considerably enhances the expressive power of functional programming languages. The programmer is allowed to define polymorphic functions in HOPE by using type variables in the "dec" statement for a function. In HOPE, "poly" might be declared in either of the following ways:

```
typevar alpha
dec poly : truval # alpha # alpha  -> alpha
--- poly(a,b,c) <= b if a else c                    (P1)

typevar alpha
dec poly : truval # alpha # alpha  -> alpha
--- poly(a,b,c) <= a then b else c                  (P2)
```

The hash (#) symbol, which denotes Cartesian product, is used to separate the different parameter types of functions taking more than one parameter. The two definitions are equivalent and illustrate the two different forms of conditional expression. Both definitions use a type variable "alpha". The declarations of "poly" specify that, for any application, the second two parameters must be of the same type and that the result will be of the same type as the parameters. The actual type is determined at the point that "poly" is applied and may be different for different applications. Thus (P1) and (P2) go some way towards encapsulating the semantics of the SUGAR definition. However, in the SUGAR version, "b" and "c" can have arbitrary types and need not be of the same type. It is tempting to define the HOPE function as shown below:

```
typevar alpha, beta, gamma
dec poly : truval # alpha # beta  -> gamma
--- poly(a,b,c) <= b if a else c                    (P3)
```

There are two problems with this definition. The first problem is that the declaration of "poly" is now too general. The declaration says that the second two parameters of "poly" may be of different types and that "poly" produces a result that has some arbitrary type. It is clear to us that "gamma" must be the same as either "alpha" or "beta" but the declaration does not say this. Instead of "gamma", we need a union type, union(alpha, beta), as in ALGOL-68; we shall see later how HOPE data declarations may be used to achieve this effect. A more serious problem is that the polymorphic type checker used in

HOPE enforces the rule that both branches of a conditional expression must have the same type and (P3) infringes this when "alpha" and "beta" are instantiated to different types.

A further difference arises from the fact that SUGAR definitions define curried functions. Thus the SUGAR version of "poly" can be used with either a complete set of parameters or with some subset of its parameters; in particular, we can make the following definition:

```
K is poly(true);    # the K combinator #
```

The equivalent HOPE definition would be rejected because the Cartesian product in the declaration indicates that all parameters are required in an application. If a function is to be used in the way illustrated above it must be explicitly declared as a curried function:

```
dec polyc : truval  -> (alpha  -> (alpha  -> alpha))
--- polyc(a)  <= lambda b =>
              lambda c => a then b else c
```

The expression defining "polyc(a)" shows the HOPE representation for unnamed functions (λ-expressions).

It may appear that we are suggesting that HOPE lacks some of the expressive power of SUGAR. While this is superficially true, the issue of typing is an extremely important consideration in software engineering. The typing features of HOPE allow complete compile-time type checking without putting too much of a burden on the programmer. This will be extremely important when parallel machines are used to execute functional programs because of the difficulty of tracing run-time errors in these machines. It is inevitable that there will be a price for the increased reliability of HOPE programs and we feel that this has been kept to a reasonable minimum.

8.3.2 Data Abstraction

In the last subsection we introduced some of the built-in types of HOPE. It is also possible for the programmer to define new types. A type is characterized by a set of constructors. For example, the data type "num" has two constructors associated with it; the nullary constructor 0 and the successor constructor. A new type is introduced by a "data" statement, for example "num" could be defined as follows:

```
data num == 0 ++ succ(num)
```

Thus the elements of "num" are 0, succ(0), succ(succ(0)), etc. The built-in type "num" allows the user to use a shorthand form for these elements (0, 1, 2, etc.). In general, any data type will consist of at least one nullary constructor (a primitive object of the type) and one or more other constructors. Another example is the "stack of numbers" data type which has two constructors, the empty stack and the "push" constructor that allows us to add another number to the head of the stack:

```
data stack == empty ++ push(num,stack)
```

It is likely that we will want to use stacks with different types, for example a stack of characters. The way we defined "stack" above would preclude this use and we would have to define a new data type "stack of characters". Alternatively, we could use a type variable to define a more general type:

```
typevar alpha
data stack(alpha) == empty ++ push(alpha,stack(alpha))
```

This data declaration introduces a whole new family of types, two instances of which are "stack(num)" (equivalent to the type defined above) and "stack(char)".

When one defines a type, one normally requires some accessor, or observer, functions as well as the constructors. For example, we probably would need a "pop" function to remove an element from the top of a stack and a "top" function to access the top element. Having introduced the data type, the accessors can be defined in the usual way:

```
typevar alpha
data stack(alpha) == empty ++ push(alpha,stack(alpha))
dec pop : stack(alpha) -> stack(alpha)
dec top : stack(alpha) -> alpha
--- pop(push(a,b)) <= b
--- pop(empty) <= empty
--- top(push(a,b)) <= a
--- top(empty) <= error
```

It should be noted that the constructors have been used to specify patterns in the definitions of "pop" and "top". The value delivered by "top(empty)" is the system-defined error token.

Recent research in software engineering has focused attention on the notion of data abstractions or abstract data types. A data abstraction is a type definition along with a collection of routines that may be used to manipulate items of the type. Important aspects of this approach are that implementation details are hidden from the user of the type and elements may only be accessed using the provided routines. One advantage of this approach is that the programmer can use types that are tailor-made for the application rather than having to distort the application to fit in with the system-defined types. In HOPE, a data abstraction can be defined using the module construct:

```
module stacks
typevar alpha
pubtype stack(alpha)
pubconst pop,top,empty,push
data stack(alpha) == empty ++ push(alpha,stack(alpha))
dec pop : stack(alpha) -> stack(alpha)
dec top : stack(alpha) -> alpha
--- pop(push(a,b)) <= b
--- pop(empty) <= empty
--- top(push(a,b)) <= a
--- top(empty) <= error
end
```

A module has a name, in the example it is "stacks". The module may only be accessed through its public types and constants, introduced by "pubtype" and "pubconst" respectively. Thus the internal details of the definition are effectively hidden. Before a program can use this module it must import the declaration by a "uses" statement, for example:

```
module transform
uses stacks;
      .
      .
      .
end
```

We now return to the definition of "poly" in the last subsection. We suggested that we could use data declarations to overcome an apparent restriction on the definition of polymorphic functions. The technique involves defining a union type as shown below:

```
data union(alpha,beta) == first(alpha) ++ second(beta)
```

This new type may then be used in the declaration of poly as shown:

```
dec poly : truval # alpha # beta -> union(alpha,beta)
--- poly(a,b,c) <= a then first(b) else second(c)
```

8.3.3 Other Features

There are many features of HOPE that have not been discussed in the preceding subsections. We do not attempt to give an exhaustive description of the language here; the reader is referred to the bibliography for more details. However, there are some other interesting facilities that do not relate directly to the typing features of HOPE and we briefly mention these below.

Firstly, user-defined functions can be declared as operators, allowing the user to write the function applications using one of a variety of different notations (e.g. infix or postfix). For example, to insert a number into an ordered list, we might define the function "into" as shown below:

```
dec into : num # list num -> list num
--- into(a,b::c) <= a<b then a :: (b :: c) else b :: into(a,c)
--- into(a,nil) <= a :: nil
```

where "::" is equivalent to the LISP "cons" operator. The function "into" can be declared as an infix operator and used in an expression as shown below:

```
infix into : 6
let numlis == 2 into [1,3,4]
```

The number in the "infix" statement is the priority that the "into" operator is to have. The "let" statement introduces a definition for an identifier; in its most general form the object on the left of "==" is a pattern (so that subcomponents of a structured object can be named).

HOPE has two different notations for auxiliary definitions. The first line of the definition of "into" could be rewritten in either of the following two, equivalent, ways:

```
--- into(a,d) <= let b :: c == d in
                ( a < b then a :: d else b :: into(a,c) )

--- into(a,d) <= ( a < b then a :: d else b :: into(a,c) )
                where b :: c == d
```

The extra brackets are needed to force the auxiliary definition to apply to the whole expression. If they were omitted the definition would only apply to the smallest well-formed expression after the "into" or before the "where".

Finally, the HOPE systems that are currently available use call-by-value semantics except in the case of lists of objects where the programmer has the option of specifying lazy evaluation. The following function:

```
dec from : num —> list num
--- from(n) <= n :: from(n+1)
```

would not terminate when it was applied. This is comparable to the LISP definition of "from" using the "cons" operator. However, HOPE provides a lazy "cons" function, "lcons", and if we redefine "from":

```
dec from : num —> list num
--- from(n) <= lcons(n,from(n+1))
```

then it will operate in the same way as the SUGAR function.

8.3.4 An Example

We close this section with a larger example. The program presented below is a graph reducer for combinator graphs. The reduction mechanism has "S", "K", "I", "+" and the integers as its constants and a program is represented by a binary graph as in the SK-reduction machine (see Chapter 5). We introduce a new data type to represent program graphs, called "sk", which has four constructors. There is an "empty" constructor to generate an empty "sk" graph, a "number" constructor that adds a numeric leaf, a "combop" constructor that adds an operator leaf and the general constructor "node".

```
data sk == empty ++ number(num) ++ combop(char) ++ node(sk,sk)
```

The "reduce" function takes a parameter of type "sk" and attempts to reduce it to a numeric leaf using the normal reduction rules. Below we give a top-level design of the function.

```
reduce is a function which takes one parameter, graph, of
type sk producing
    when graph is empty then empty
    when graph is a numeric leaf then the leaf
    when graph is an operator leaf then the leaf
    when graph is an application of S then the result of
        reducing a new graph generated according to the S reduction
        rule
    when graph is an application of K then result of
        reducing a new graph generated according to the K reduction
        rule
```

```
when graph is an application of I then the result of
    reducing a new graph generated according to the I reduction
    rule
when graph is a node whose left subgraph is an operator
    then the node
when graph is an application of + to two numeric leaves
    then a leaf containing the sum of the two leaves
when graph is an application of + to two subgraphs of
    which one (at least) is non-numeric then the result
    of reducing a graph corresponding to an application of
    of + to the reduced forms of its two operands
otherwise the result of reducing the graph
    created by reducing the left subgraph
```

We recall that the reduction rule for the S combinator is:

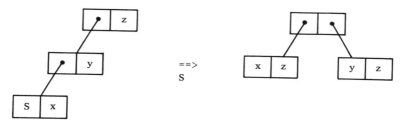

Thus a graph representing an application of S is represented as:

```
node( node( node( combop( 'S' ), x ), y ), z )
```

and the graph produced by applying the S reduction rule is:

```
node( node( x, z ), node( y, z ) )
```

The refinements of the above definition are straightforward and we go straight to the HOPE representation of "reduce"; we have reversed the order of the cases to conform with the HOPE requirement that more general cases are listed first:

```
module sk_machine;
pubtype sk;
pubconst reduce, empty, number, combop, node;
data sk == empty ++ number(num) ++ combop(char) ++
           node(sk,sk);
dec reduce : sk -> sk;
--- reduce(node(a,b)) <= reduce(node(reduce(a),b));
--- reduce(node(node(combop('+'),x),y)) <=
        reduce(node(node(combop('+'),reduce(x),reduce(y)));
--- reduce(node(node(combop('+'),number(x)),number(y))) <=
```

```
          number(x+y);
 --- reduce(node(combop(a),x)) <= node(combop(a),x);
 --- reduce(node(combop('I'),x)) <= reduce(x);
 --- reduce(node(node(combop('K'),x),y)) <= reduce(x);
 --- reduce(node(node(node(combop('S'),x),y),z)) <=
          reduce(node(node(x,z),node(y,z)));
 --- reduce(combop(op)) <= combop(op);
 --- reduce(number(a)) <= number(a);
 --- reduce(empty) <= empty;
end;
```

Before the definitions in this module can be used they have to be
imported. It is also convenient to make a series of definitions of
"combop"s.

```
uses sk_machine;
let I == combop('I');
let S == combop('S');
let K == combop('K');
let PLUS == combop('+');
```

We are now in a position to apply the "reduce" function. We use the
increment function as an example.

```
     inc = λ x. + x 1
```

```
in combinators:
     inc = S( S (K+) I ) ( K1 )
```

```
in HOPE:
     let inc == node(node(S,node(node(S,node(K,PLUS)),I)),
               node(K,number(1)));
```

An application of "reduce" might be:

```
reduce(node(inc,number(8)))
```

which would reduce to:

```
number(9)
```

Finally, it should be noted that HOPE is still evolving as
new research is done. Although the program presented above does run
on all existing HOPE implementations (with a possible reordering of
the equations), it has been criticized because the equations do not
have mutually exclusive patterns on the left hand side. It would be
possible to eradicate overlapping patterns at the expense of introducing
many more equations. However, we have chosen to present the

program as shown because it is not yet clear how HOPE will develop in this area.

EXERCISE

Write a HOPE program that converts an unordered list of numbers into an ordered tree where the leaves from left to right are in ascending order.

8.4 FP SYSTEMS

In 1977, John Backus delivered a lecture in which he posed the question: "Can programming be liberated from the von Neumann style?" [Bac]. He pointed out that over the previous twenty years languages had been getting bigger (in fact he described them as fat and flabby), and he identified the root cause as the close correlation between the concepts of conventional languages and the structure of machines based on the von Neumann model.

We are familiar with the notion that it is theoretically possible to eliminate variables altogether, since we have seen that this can be achieved by the use of combinators. Backus suggests that it is practicable to use a programming language without (or almost without) variables, thus relieving the programmer of the need to name intermediate values generated during computations. The only use he would retain for variables is as names for useful functions which could be entered into a library and stored for use in later programs. He also suggests that languages which allow the definition of functions of all higher orders, for example the λ-calculus, are in some sense too powerful a formalism, and that what we need is a set of atomic objects and primitive functions over those objects, or over vectors of those objects, together with a set of combining forms which allow the construction of further functions over the same domain. His idea is that by restricting the combining forms in this way, we would become very familiar with their properties, and we could develop programs by starting with simple but possibly inefficient definitions of functions which are then manipulated into more efficient definitions, correctness being maintained by the use of transformations, each of which preserve partial correctness.

8.4.1 Definitions

Systems such as those described above, Backus has called Functional Programming systems (FP systems). In order to define a particular FP system, we must specify a set of Atoms, from which we can derive the set of Objects, a set of Primitive Functions over the Objects, and a set of Combining Forms, from which we can derive the set of Definable Functions.

```
FP systems

given a set of Atoms, the set of Objects consists of:

    ⊥, the undefined Object (called "bottom"),
    the set of Atoms,
    all vectors over (Objects - {⊥});

given a set of Primitive Functions and a set of Combining Forms,
the set of Definable Functions consists of:

    the Primitive Functions, each of which must be a strict
        function from Objects to Objects,
    all functions C(f₁, f₂, ..., fₙ), for C a Combining Form,
        each of f₁, f₂, ..., fₙ a Definable Function, or Object,
        where n must be suitable for C, and C must produce
        only strict functions from Objects to Objects,
    all functions f, given by an equation of the form f = E(f),
        where E(f) is a functional form, constructed  by
        applying Combining Forms to Definable Functions and
        the function symbol f;

there is a single operation called application, which given a
Definable Function and an Object, produces the result of applying
the Function to the Object.
```

We shall take as our set of Atoms for the purposes of the following illustrations of FP systems the set of integers in normal decimal digit notation, together with the set of all finite, non-empty strings of upper-case letters.

```
Examples of FP Objects

given the set of Atoms defined as:

    Atoms = the set of decimal integers with optional minus sign
            together with the set of upper-case letter sequences
```

here are some examples of Atoms:

ABC, 1983, 0, −55, YES, NO

here are some examples of Objects:

$\perp$, YES, 123, <−1, 0, 1>, < <CAT, GATO>, <DOG, PERRO> >, < >

Note that the Atoms YES and NO will be given the significance "true" and "false" respectively.

We now give examples of Primitive Functions, using the design language to explain their effect. All Primitive Functions must map $\perp$ to $\perp$, so we consider only non-$\perp$ arguments. We will use as symbols for Primitive Functions strings which can be distinguished from Atoms, such as $+$, $*$, transpose, sel_1.

Examples of Primitive Functions

```
atom      [x] when x is an Atom then YES,
              otherwise NO

null      [x] when x = < > then YES, otherwise NO

hd        [x] when atom(x) then ⊥,
              when x = < > then ⊥,
              when x is of form <x₁, ... xₙ> then x₁

tl        [x] when atom(x) then ⊥,
              when x = < > then ⊥,
              when x is of form <x₁> then < >,
              when x is of form <x₁, x₂, ... xₙ> then <x₂, ... xₙ>

sel_n     where n is a positive integer ( for example sel_1, sel_2 )
          [x] when x is of form <x₁, ... xₘ> and (m>n or m=n) then
                  xₙ,
              otherwise ⊥

id        [x] x

eq        [x] when x is of form <x₁, x₂> then x₁ = x₂,
              otherwise ⊥

gt        [x] when x is of form <x₁, x₂>,
                          where x₁, x₂ numeric then x₁ > x₂,
              otherwise ⊥

ge, le, ne, lt
          defined similarly to mean greater than or equal to,
          less than or equal to, not equal to, less than
```

$+$ [x] when x is of form $\langle x_1, x_2 \rangle$,
                       and both x_1, x_2 are numbers then $x_1 + x_2$,
           otherwise $\perp$

$*$, $-$, $/$
           defined similarly, changing $+$ to $*$, $-$, $/$ respectively

rev   [x] when atom(x) then $\perp$,
              when x = < > then < >,
              when x is of form $\langle x_1, x_2, \ldots x_n \rangle$ then $\langle x_n, \ldots x_2, x_1 \rangle$

distl   [x] when x is of form $\langle y, < > \rangle$ then < >,
              when x is of form $\langle y, \langle x_1, x_2, \ldots x_n \rangle \rangle$ then
                 $\langle \langle y, x_1 \rangle, \langle y, x_2 \rangle, \ldots \langle y, x_n \rangle \rangle$,
              otherwise $\perp$

distr   [x] when x is of form $\langle < >, y \rangle$ then < >,
              when x is of form $\langle \langle x_1, x_2, \ldots x_n \rangle, y \rangle$ then
                 $\langle \langle x_1, y \rangle, \langle x_2, y \rangle, \ldots \langle x_n, y \rangle \rangle$,
              otherwise $\perp$

transpose
           [x] when x is of form
                      $\langle \langle x_{11}, x_{12}, \ldots x_{1n} \rangle,$
                        $\langle x_{21}, x_{22}, \ldots x_{2n} \rangle,$
                        $\ldots$
                        $\langle x_{m1}, x_{m2}, \ldots x_{mn} \rangle \rangle$ then
                                           $\langle \langle x_{11}, x_{21}, \ldots x_{m1} \rangle,$
                                             $\langle x_{12}, x_{22}, \ldots x_{m2} \rangle,$
                                             $\ldots$
                                             $\langle x_{1n}, x_{2n}, \ldots x_{mn} \rangle \rangle$,
              otherwise $\perp$

and   [x] when x = <YES, YES> then YES,
              when x = <YES, NO> or <NO, YES> or <NO, NO> then NO,
              otherwise $\perp$

or   [x] when x = <YES, YES> or <YES, NO> or <NO, YES> then YES,
              when x = <NO, NO> then NO,
              otherwise $\perp$

not   [x] when x = YES then NO,
              when x = NO then YES,
              otherwise $\perp$

apndl   [x] when x is of form $\langle y, < > \rangle$ then $\langle y \rangle$,
              when x is of form $\langle y, \langle x_1, \ldots x_n \rangle \rangle$
                                           then $\langle y, x_1, \ldots x_n \rangle$,
              otherwise $\perp$

apndr   [x] when x is of form $< < >, y>$ then $<y>$,
         when x is of form $< <x_1, \ldots x_n>, y>$
                                        then $<x_1, \ldots x_n, y>$,
         otherwise $\perp$

selr_n   where n is a positive integer,
         [x] sel_n(rev(x))

tlr   [x] when x is of form $<x_1, \ldots x_n, y>$ then $<x_1, \ldots x_n>$,
         when x is of form $<y>$ then $< >$,
         otherwise $\perp$

iota   [n] when n is a positive integer then $<1, 2, \ldots n>$,
         otherwise $\perp$

Next we give examples of Combining Forms, and again we use the design notation to describe the effects of these higher order functions which in general will take functions from Objects to Objects as parameters:

Examples of Combining Forms

composition
         $[f_1, f_2, \ldots f_n]$ ([x] f_1 (f_2 ($\ldots f_n(x) \ldots$)))

    we use the notation: f_1 o f_2 o $\ldots$ o f_n

construction
         $[f_1, \ldots f_n]$ ([x] $< f_1(x), \ldots f_n(x) >$)

    we use the notation: $[f_1, \ldots f_n]$

choice
         [test, yeschoice, nochoice]
                ([x] when test(x) = YES then yeschoice(x),
                    when test(x) = NO then nochoice(x),
                    otherwise $\perp$
)

    we use the notation: (test --> yeschoice, nochoice)

application to each element of a vector
         [f] ([x] when x = $< >$ then $< >$,
                when x is of form $<x_1, \ldots x_n>$
                            then $< f(x_1), \ldots f(x_n) >$,
                otherwise $\perp$
)

    we use the notation: toall-f

left insertion
       [f] ([x] when x is of form <y> then y,
                  when x is of form $<x_1, .. x_n, y>$ then
                       f(< (leftinsert(f) ($<x_1, ... x_n>$)), y>),
                  otherwise ⊥
)

       where f must be a function from <Object, Object> to Object;
       gives the effect of left association for vectors with more
       than two elements;
       we use the notation: insl-f

right insertion
       [f] ([x] when x is of form <y> then y,
                  when x is of form $<y, x_1, .. x_n>$ then
                       f(<y, (rightinsert(f) ($<x_1, ... x_n>$)) >),
                  otherwise ⊥
)

       where f must be a function from <Object, Object> to Object;
       gives the effect of right association;
       we use the notation: insr-f

constant
       [x] ([y] x)

       where x is an Object;
       we use the notation: #x

For ease of reference, we give a summary of the notation for
Combining Forms:

Notation for Combining Forms

f_1 o f_2 o ... f_n
       composition of functions f_1, f_2, ... f_n

$[f_1, f_2, ... f_n]$
       construction applied to f_1, f_2, ... f_n

(test --> yeschoice, nochoice)
       choice applied to functions test, yeschoice and nochoice

toall-f
       represents the function which applies f to all elements of
       a given vector

insl-f
       left insertion applied to f

```
insr-f
      right insertion applied to f

#x
      the constant function which yields Object x for all inputs
```

Clearly we would like to be able to give names to certain Definable Functions, and this is done by means of Definitions, as we see below:

Examples of Definitions

```
      Def sum ≡ (null --> #0, insr-+)

      Def len ≡ (null --> #0, + o [#1, len o tl] )

      Def member ≡ insr-or  o  toall-eq  o  distl

      Def elemcount ≡  sum  o  toall-(#1)
```

A Definition may have a right hand side which is a functional form which uses Combining Forms, other Definable Functions, possibly referring to them by name, and the symbol which is being defined. There should be at most one Definition for any given symbol, and of course the names used in Definitions should not clash with those of Primitive Functions.

Having given some Definitions within an FP system, we will want to apply functions we have defined to Objects; we use the notation "f:x" to mean the application of function f to Object x. Note once again that the Definable Functions are all first order functions, that is, they must be applied to Objects and deliver Objects; this is so because the Primitive Functions are themselves of this kind, and all the Combining Forms are such that they only yield functions of this kind, when given such functions as arguments. In order to define the semantics of an FP system, we need to know how to apply any Definable Function f to any Object x.

Semantics of FP systems

```
to apply function f to object x

      when x is ⊥, result is ⊥,
      when f is a Primitive Function,
          then apply that Primitive Function to x,
      when f is a functional form,
          then the description of that form tells how to
          apply f, in terms of the parameters of the form,
```

```
when f is the name of a Definable Function,
     occurring as the symbol defined by a Definition,
     then apply the right hand side of that Definition
     to x,
otherwise, result is ⊥
```

As an example of application, we compute

```
"member : <4, <1, 4, 9>>"
```

where member is defined as above:

```
member : <4, <1, 4, 9>>

     ==> insr-or o toall-eq o distl : <4, <1, 4, 9>>

     ==> insr-or o toall-eq : <<4, 1>, <4, 4>, <4, 9>>

     ==> insr-or : <NO, YES, NO>

     ==> or : <NO, or : <YES, NO>>

     ==> or : <NO, YES>

     ==> YES
```

8.4.2 Developing Programs in FP Systems

Within FP systems it is possible to define functions recursively, in a way which is familiar to us from SUGAR or LISP, but it is often possible to replace an explicitly recursive definition by a functional form which has the same effect, but which does not refer to the symbol which is being defined. The two functions "len" and "elemcount" defined above, for example, are in fact the same function; given an Object which is a vector of Objects, they each compute the length of that vector. However, the function "len" is defined in the obvious recursive way, whereas the function "elemcount" is defined in terms of Primitive Functions and Combining Forms, and makes no reference to its own name on the right hand side. Though this second definition looks rather strange initially, in fact it expresses the equally obvious solution to the problem of computing the length of a vector; it says that we map each element of the vector into 1, and then add up the 1's. Now there may be some advantage in a definition which is not explicitly recursive, because we can reason about it directly, using algebraic rules which apply to the Combining Forms and Primitive

Functions of the FP system we are using, whereas in the case of explicit recursion, we have only an equation for the function concerned, which will make any reasoning about that function more intricate.

A distinct advantage of the non-recursive style for the programmer is illustrated here. Once the function "sum" has been defined, it can be used as a building block for more complex definitions, as it has been in "elemcount"; any function which requires that we perform the same function on each of the elements of a vector, and then add up the results can now be written without having to use explicit tail recursion. For example, the sum of the squares, "sumsq", could be defined as follows:

```
Def sumsq ≡ sum  o  toall-(* o [id, id])
```

Now we will develop the definition of a slightly more significant example. We want a function "parsums" which, given a vector of integers, say $\langle x_1, \ldots x_n \rangle$, produces a vector of integers, say $\langle y_1, \ldots y_n \rangle$, such that

```
for each i, 1 <= i <= n,
y_i = the sum of x_1, x_2, ... x_i
```

Now we start from the observation that

```
parsums : <x_1, x_2, ... x_n, y>
        = apndr : < parsums : <x_1, x_2, ... x_n>, <p_n + y> >

where p_n is the last element of parsums : <x_1, x_2, ... x_n>,
that is, p_n = selr_1 : ( parsums : <x_1, x_2, ... x_n> )
```

This can be expressed as

```
parsums : <x_1, x_2, ... x_n, y>
        = parapndr : < parsums : <x_1, x_2, ... x_n>, y>

where parapndr ≡ apndr o [ sel_1, + o [selr_1 o sel_1, sel_2] ]
```

So it would seem that we have to leftinsert this function "parapndr" in order to compute "parsums". But this is not quite correct since

```
insl-parapndr : <x>  =  x
```

so that the leftinsertion process does not get started up as it should. The problem is that "parapndr" needs a vector as its left operand. We need to amend the given vector, so that its first element is itself a vector. We claim that, for $n \geq 1$,

```
parsums: <x₁, ... x_n> = insl-parapndr : < <x₁>, ... x_n>
```

We proceed by induction on n:

```
case n = 1:-

    parsums: <x₁> = <x₁>
            (by definition of parsums);

    insl-parapndr : < <x₁> > = <x₁>
            (by definition of insl-)

case n = m+1:-

    parsums : <x₁, ... x_m, x_n>
            = parapndr : < parsums : <x₁, ... x_m>, x_n>
                    (definition of parsums and parapndr)
            = parapndr : < insl-parapndr : < <x₁>, ... x_m>, x_n>
                    (inductive assumption)
            = insl-parapndr : < <x₁, ... x_m, x_n>
                    (definition of insl-)
```

Now we can see how to define "parsums"; given $< >$, presumably we want $< >$ as result; given $<x_1, ... x_n>$, $n \geq 1$, we must change this to $<<x_1>, ... x_n>$, and then apply the function insl-parapndr to the result of this. This gives us the Definitions:

```
Def parapndr ≡ apndr o [ sel_1, + o [selr_1 o sel_1, sel_2] ]

Def parsums ≡ (null --> #< >,
               insl-parapndr  o  apndl  o  [ [hd], tl ] )
```

8.4.3 FFP Systems

As we have described FP systems, any particular system has a fixed set of Combining Forms, which we assume are implemented in some way external to the FP system, as are the Primitive Functions. Unless we have some way of remembering Definitions, an FP system is essentially a fixed entity, whose limits are set by the choice of Primitive Functions and Combining Forms. Clearly it is desirable to have some way of specifying Combining Forms which does not depend on an external specification language; with this in mind, Backus proposes systems which he calls FFP systems (Formal Functional Programming systems). The basic domain is extended to include applications, and so consists of Atoms, Objects and Applications, and vectors constructed from these. The elements of this domain are called Expressions. Some of the Atoms are used as names for Primitive Functions. The syntax of an FFP system is very much like that of LISP, except that application is made explicit; the application of "f" to "x" is represented by (f:x), rather than (f x) as it would be in LISP. The semantics of FFP systems are very similar to those of FLISP, except that an extra rule is required to describe the effect of application of a vector to an Expression. This rule, called the metacomposition rule, is what allows the system to define Combining Forms; each Combining Form is represented in the system by a suitable vector which combines Atoms representing Primitive Functions in a way which produces the desired effect, in combination with the metacomposition rule. The rule also allows us to define Combining Forms and Definable Functions recursively, without the need for an environment-maintaining mechanism. In effect we abstract function names out of functional forms, just as we did in order to derive combinator expressions in Chapter 5.

Backus also addresses the issue of history sensitivity; clearly we want a systematic way of including useful definitions of functions in a library of functions, which can be preserved for use in later sessions. A facility is suggested that allows us to fetch a function from the library by giving the name by which the library knows that function, which then has the same effect as definition of that function. Of course, we also need the facility to store a given definition in the library under some chosen name. This kind of facility is often available in existing LISP systems, in cooperation with the file-system of the host machine.

Whatever the theoretical virtues of the FP style of programming, the authors have found that the lack of a local definition facility is a considerable disadvantage, and one also frequently finds oneself very constrained by the set of Combining Forms available. In an FFP system it seems that one would find it convenient to define new Combining Forms as each new problem was tackled, thus undermining the notion that one should use a small set of Combining Forms whose properties would thereby become very familiar.

We will not carry further our discussion of FFP systems, but the reader is referred to Williams [Wil] for further information.

8.4.4 An Implementation of an FP System in FLISP

So that the reader can sample the flavor of FP systems, we have written an implementation of an FP system in FLISP, the details of which will be found in Appendix 4. We have adopted the FLISP form of function invocation, that is, the name of a function or of a combining form appears as the first Elem of a Brack, which means that the syntax is not so convenient as we might wish. As examples, we give the translation of the definitions given earlier in this section:

```
(defp 'sum (choose 'null (const 0) (insr '+)))
```

> note: defp causes an FP Definition to be made,
> choose, const, insr are the names for the Combining Forms
> choice, constant and right insertion respectively;
> we assume that 'Elem can be used as a shorthand for
> (quote Elem), and that certain operator symbols such
> as + can be used as Atoms.

```
(defp 'len (choose 'null (const 0)
               (compose '+ (construct (list (const 1)
                                   (compose 'len 'tl)))))
)
```

> note: compose and construct are Combining Forms,
> but compose accepts only two inputs; compo3 is provided
> for composition of three functions, and obviously further
> such Forms could be defined; construct takes only one
> argument which must be a Brack whose Elems are the
> components required.

```
(defp 'member
      (compo3 (insr 'orr) (toall 'eqq) 'distl)
)
```

> note: "orr" and "eqq" are used to avoid confusion with or
> and eq which will normally be system-defined functions in
> the LISP implementation.

```
(defp 'elemcount
      (compose 'sum (toall (const 1)))
)
```

```
(defp 'sumsq
      (compose 'sum (toall (compose '* (construct '(id id)))))
)
```

```
(defp 'parapndr
      (compose 'apndr
        (construct (list (sel 1)
                   (compose '+
                     (construct (list (compose (selr 1) (sel 1))
                                 (sel 2)))))))
)
```

> note: sel 1, sel 2, etc. are used to represent

sel_1, sel_2, etc., that is, sel is a Combining Form,
which takes the place of an infinite set of Primitive
Functions; similarly, selr_n is represented by selr n.

```
(defp 'parsums
        (choose 'null (const nil)
                (compo3 (insl 'parapndr)
                     'apndl (construct (list (construct '(hd)) 'tl)))))
)
```

It will be seen that we can introduce new Combining Forms just
as easily as Primitive Functions by giving suitable FLISP Definitions.
Indeed, the implementation we have here is in some ways rather like
the FFP systems described in Backus [Bac]. The main difference is
that, since it is based on an existing LISP implementation, we can use
the underlying environment mechanism to keep track of the names of
functions and their corresponding definitions. So, for example, we do
not need an abstraction mechanism nor the metacomposition rule in
order to handle explicit mutual recursion.

EXERCISES

1. Write a definition in our FP system of a function "primes" which
given a single positive integer greater than 2, produces the vector
which consists of all the prime numbers less than and possibly
including that integer. You should first define auxiliary functions
"sieve" and "filter" analogous to those given in the primes program in
SUGAR in Chapter 2.

2. Write a definition, and any necessary auxiliary definitions, for a
function "cart" which given an Object of the form:

$$< vec_1, vec_2, \ldots vec_n >$$

where each of vec_1 to vec_n is a vector of Objects, will produce the cartesian
product vector, each of whose elements is a vector which consists of
one Object chosen from each of vec_1 to vec_n in that order. It may be helpful
to define first a function "cart2" which performs the same function for
Objects of the form

$$< vec_1, vec_2 >$$

and then generalize this. (Note: Williams discusses this function in

[Wil].)

3. Suppose we want to define a function "perms" which given a vector will produce the vector consisting of all the permutations of the elements of the given vector. We show a method by example. Suppose the given vector is (1 2 3); then, consider the following sequence of transformations:

```
(1 2 3)
((1 2 3) (1 2 3))
((1 (1 2 3)) (2 (1 2 3)) (3 (1 2 3)))
((1 (2 3)) (2 (1 3)) (3 (1 2)))
((1 perms:(2 3)) (2 perms:(1 3)) (3 perms:(1 2)))
```

and then, assuming that perms computes correctly for vectors of length 2, we get

```
((1 ((2 3) (3 2))) (2 ((1 3) (3 1))) (3 ((1 2) (2 1))))
```

and continuing our series of transformations

```
(((1 (2 3)) (1 (3 2))) ((2 (1 3)) (2 (3 1))) ((3 (1 2)) (3 (2 1))))
(((1 2 3) (1 3 2)) ((2 1 3) (2 3 1)) ((3 1 2) (3 2 1)))
((1 2 3) (1 3 2) (2 1 3) (2 3 1) (3 1 2) (3 2 1))
```

By considering what functions are needed in the general case to achieve each of the transformations shown, write a definition of perms in our FP system.

8.5 CONCLUDING REMARKS

While the languages dealt with in this chapter are certainly more expressive than SUGAR or LISP, they still appear to be deficient in certain respects. It is clear that these languages provide a powerful notation for expressing solutions to "mathematical" problems but what about the other sorts of problems that we use computers to solve? Many problems have an applicative kernel embedded in code that handles the real-time interaction with the user. The handling of input/output and non-determinism (particularly in the operating system context) are areas of active research within the functional programming community. (See Henderson's paper in [Dar] for example.) We briefly look at the putative solutions to each of these problems.

A widely adopted solution to the problem of interactive input/output involves a simple extension to the lazy evaluation mechanism and does not necessitate any syntactic change to the languages. Each device is associated with a lazy list, devices which are bi-directional, such as discs, are considered to be equivalent to two uni-directional devices. In a typed language the type of the list associated with a device would determine the type of items that could be input or output; in this case the lists would be constructed from items of a single type but we will use SUGAR, a type free language, and allow heterogeneous lists, particularly for output, as this clarifies the exposition. A request for input from a device is either satisfied immediately because the input was already present, or may cause execution to be suspended until the input has been produced. As output is generated, it is appended to the appropriate list and may be physically output as soon as it has been produced (i.e. before the whole list has been constructed). A simple interactive program is shown below:

```
screen is { double(keyboard)
            where
            double is [in] if in = <> then <>
                            else ((hd in): "times two is") &&
                            (2 * (hd in)): nl: double(tl in)
                            endf
            };
```

The program receives numeric input from the keyboard, doubles each number and outputs it with some appropriate text on the screen.

A program is non-deterministic if it has the property that its output is not solely dependent on its inputs. Other factors that might play a role in determining the output are such unpredictable things as the relative time of arrival of inputs from different sources. The formal semantics of non-determinism are by no means as simple as for the deterministic case and the mathematical foundations of non-determinism are still an area of active research. The addition of non-determinism to functional languages appears to destroy the applicative nature of the languages by invalidating the property of referential transparency. (This need not be so if we allow names to be associated with sets of values where each element of the set represents a different possible outcome.) An important issue in non-determinism is the issue of "fairness". A system that supports non-determinism is said to be fair if given two objects that potentially consume infinite resources (e.g. sources producing infinite input lists), neither object is held up for an infinite time waiting for the resource. Henderson and others have proposed the addition of a non-deterministic operator to functional languages. The operator is called "merge" and it produces a fair interleaving of values from two lists. Returning to our earlier example, if we have two keyboards driving the˙same screen, we could rewrite our program as shown below:

```
screen is { double( merge( keyboard1, keyboard2 ) )
```

This would produce an arbitrary interleaving of the outputs produced from the two inputs. It would be possible to "tag" inputs from the two keyboards so that the output from each could be differentiated (see Henderson).

Finally, we briefly describe another approach, relational programming, that has become linked with functional programming. An umbrella term that covers both approaches is "declarative programming" and declarative programming forms a cornerstone of the current research into "Fifth Generation" computers. Our purpose here is to explain the relationship between the two styles of programming, the functional and the relational.

While the two approaches do have many superficial similarities — both classes of languages are non-procedural and, in their pure forms, involve programming without side-effects — they do have different mathematical foundations. In writing functional programs, the programmer is concerned with specifying the solution to a problem as a collection of many-to-one transformations. This corresponds closely to the mathematical definition of a function. On the other hand, a relational program specifies a collection of many-to-many transformations. Thus in relational programming languages, there is a set of solutions to a particular application rather than the single solution that is produced from a function application.

An example will serve to clarify some of these points. A simple relation from everyday life is the "is the brother of" relationship which may be partially defined as below:

```
Joe is the brother of Jack
Jack is the brother of Fred
Joe is the brother of Fred
```

Notice that the relation maps "Joe" to two different siblings; this would not be permitted in a functional language. A straightforward use of the relation is shown below:

```
Joe is the brother of Who?
```

which would produce two answers "Jack" and "Fred". Another interesting facility provided in some relational languages is that relations can be used "backwards" so that the following is perfectly valid:

```
Who is the brother of Fred?
```

which, as expected, produces the two answers "Jack" and "Joe".

The execution mechanisms that have been proposed for relational programming languages are radically different from the approaches that we have discussed for functional programming languages. Although some of the parallel implementations do produce a complete solution set, the traditional approach has been for the machine or interpreter to produce a single solution and to use "backtracking" if further solutions are required.

One particular example of a relational programming language is PROLOG, a language that was invented at the University of Marseilles in 1973. PROLOG is based on first order logic and a program is a series of logical clauses. We illustrate a set of simple clauses so that the reader might gain some idea of the differences between relational and functional programming. The clauses beginning with "app" tell us how to concatenate two lists and the clauses beginning with "rev" tell us how to reverse a list.

```
app([],X,X).
app([X | Y],Z,[X | W]) :- app(Y,Z,W).

rev([],[]).
rev([X | Y],Z) :- rev(Y,W), app(W,[X],Z).
```

The upper case letters are examples of PROLOG variables. These clauses are applied by asking the system to prove a new clause that involves one or other of the predicates (app and rev). Before illustrating a series of applications we show how the above clauses should be read.

```
appending the empty list to any other list X produces the
list X.
appending a list with head X and tail Y to a list Z produces
a list with head X and tail W IF appending Y to Z produces W.

reversing the empty list produces the empty list.
reversing a list with head X and tail Y produces Z IF
reversing Y produces W AND appending W to the singleton
```

```
list X produces Z.
```

Typical uses of these clauses are shown below.

```
rev([1,2,3],X).
app([1,2],[3,4],X).

rev(Y,[3,2,1]).
app(X,Y,[1,2,3,4]).
```

The first two uses are straightforward; in proving each of these clauses, PROLOG will cause the variable X to be "instantiated" to an appropriate value (in the first case [3,2,1] and in the second case [1,2,3,4]). The second two clauses are more interesting and illustrate the true capabilities of relational programming. In the first case, PROLOG uses the clauses "backwards" to instantiate Y to [1,2,3]; in the second case, PROLOG will generate the following solution set.

```
X = []                    Y = [1,2,3,4]
X = [1]                   Y = [2,3,4]
X = [1,2]                 Y = [3,4]
X = [1,2,3]               Y = [4]
X = [1,2,3,4]             Y = []
```

This contrasts with the situation in functional languages, such as KRC, where the definitions, although they look similar to the PROLOG clauses, may only be used in the "forward" direction.

```
app [] x = x
app (x : y) z = x : (app y z)

rev [] = []
rev (x : y) = app (rev y) [x]
```

There is clearly much work to be done before declarative programming languages will be able to challenge the supremacy of the imperative languages. We hope that we have given the reader some reason for feeling that the effort is worthwhile.

BIBLIOGRAPHY

In Darlington et al. there is a chapter by Turner on KRC and also an introduction to FP written by Williams. A definition of HOPE is to be found in Burstall et al. The notion of FP systems was introduced by

John Backus in his 1977 Turing Award lecture. Henderson's approach to interactive input/output and non-determinism in functional languages is also to be found in Darlington et al. Clocksin and Mellish provide a readable introduction to PROLOG and Kowalski treats logic and relational programming at a more abstract level. Clark and McCabe describe micro-PROLOG, which is a variant of PROLOG available on several micro-processors; the book also examines several application areas for logic programming.

[Bac] Backus J.W. "Can Programming be Liberated from the von Neumann Style? A Functional Style and its Algebra of Programs", Communications of the ACM, Vol. 21, pp. 613-641, August 1978.

[Bu2] Burstall R.M., McQueen D.B. and Sannella D.T. "HOPE : An experimental applicative language", University of Edinburgh, 1980.

[Cla] Clark K.L. and McCabe F.G. "micro-PROLOG: Programming in Logic", Prentice-Hall International, 1984.

[Clo] Clocksin W.F. and Mellish C.S. "Programming in Prolog", Springer-Verlag, 1981.

[Dar] Darlington J., Henderson P. and Turner D.A. "Functional Programming and its Applications", Cambridge University Press, 1982.

[Kow] Kowalski R. "Logic for Problem Solving", North-Holland, 1979.

[Wil] Williams J.H. "Notes on the FP style of Functional Programming", in [Dar].

APPENDIX 1: SUGAR SYNTAX AND SEMANTICS

Concrete Syntax of SUGAR

```
Program          ::=   Definition_list ;
Definition       ::=   Name  is  Expression
Expression       ::=   Literal
                     | Name
                     | ( Expression  )
                     | if Expression then Expression Alternatives
                     | <  Element_list  >  |  <>
                     | "  Char_list   "   |   ""
                     | Expression  ( Expression_list  )
                     | Op  Expression
                     | Expression  Op  Expression
                     | { Expression  where  Definition_list }
                     | [  Formal_list  ]  Expression
Alternatives     ::=   else Expression endf
                     | elsf Expression then Expression Alternatives
                     | endf
Formal           ::=   Name
Element          ::=   Expression
Definition_list  ::=   Definition
                     | Definition  ;  Definition_list
Element_list     ::=   Element
                     | Element  ,  Element_list
Formal_list      ::=   Formal
                     | Formal  ,  Formal_list
Name             ::=   Letter
                     | Name Letter
                     | Name Digit
                     | Name  _
Literal          ::=   Number
                     | Number  .  Number
                     | Number  e  Number
                     | '  Char
                     | true  |  false
```

In addition to the above, layout and comments (enclosed in #'s)
are permitted anywhere.

215

SUGAR operators

Numeric:	+	unary plus and binary addition
	—	unary minus and binary subtraction
	*	multiplication
	/	real division
	%	integer division
	rem	remainder after division
	<	less than
	>	greater than
	<=	less than or equal to
	>=	greater than or equal to
	=	equals
	!=	not equal to
Character:	=	equals
	!=	not equal to
Boolean:	and	
	or	
	not	unary negation
	=	equals
	!=	not equal to
Lists:	&&	concatenation of two lists
	:	prefixes the first operand to the second which must be a list
	hd	the first element of a list
	tl	the list with the first element removed
	atom	a predicate that is true if its operand is not a list
	=	equals
	!=	not equal to

Semantics

Syntactic Domains

Def	definitions
Exp	expressions
Ide	identifiers
Con	constants
Ops	operators
Lis	lists
Alt	alternatives

Abstract Syntax

$$D ::= I = E \mid I = E ; D$$

$$E ::= E \textbf{ where } D \mid$$
$$\quad C \mid I \mid \textbf{if } E \textbf{ then } E' A \mid$$
$$\quad O E \mid E O E' \mid$$
$$\quad < L > \mid <> \mid$$
$$\quad E (E') \mid I.E$$

$$L ::= E \mid E , L$$

$$A ::= \textbf{else } E \textbf{ endf} \mid \textbf{elsf } E \textbf{ then } E' A \mid \textbf{endf}$$

Semantic Domains

Env = Ide $\rightarrow$ Dev	environments
Bas = Int + Real + Char + Bool	basic values
Prm	primitive operators
Dev = Bas + Dev* + [Dev $\rightarrow$ Dev]	denotable values

Semantic Functions

OP :	Ops $\rightarrow$ Prm
CB :	Con $\rightarrow$ Bas
ED :	Exp $\rightarrow$ Env $\rightarrow$ Dev
LD :	Lis $\rightarrow$ Env $\rightarrow$ Dev*
DE :	Def $\rightarrow$ Env $\rightarrow$ Env
AD :	Alt $\rightarrow$ Env $\rightarrow$ Dev

Semantic Equations

```
ED[ E where D ]R = ED[ E ]( DE[ D ]R )
ED[ C ]R = CB[ C ]
ED[ I ]R = R( I )
ED[ if E then E' A ]R
                   = if boolean( ED[ E ]R )
                      then if ED[ E ]R
                              then ED[ E' ]R
                              else AD[ A ]R
                      else error
ED[ O E ]R = OP[ O ] ED[ E ]R
ED[ E O E' ]R = OP[ O ] ED[ E ]R ED[ E' ]R
ED[ < L > ]R = LD[ L ]R
ED[ <> ]R = nil
ED[ E ( E' ) ]R = if function( ED[ E ]R )
                   then ED[ E ]R ED[ E' ]R
                   else if list( ED[ E ]R )
                          then ED[ E ]R ↓ ED[ E' ]R
                          else error
ED[ I . E ]R = λ x . ED[ E ]R[ x / I ]

LD[ E ]R = ED[ E ]R <> nil
LD[ E , L ]R = ED[ E ]R <> LD[ L ]R

AD[ else E endf ]R = ED[ E ]R
AD[ elsf E then E' A ]R =
        ED[ if E then E' A ]R
AD[ endf ]R = error

OP[ hd ] = λ x. x    1
OP[ tl ] = λ x. tail x
OP[ : ] = λ xy. x <> y
OP[ && ] = fix λ fxy . if x = nil then y
 ]λ                    else x    1 <> (f (tail x) y)
OP[ atom ] = λ x. if list(x) then false else true


DE[ I = E ]R = R[ fix( λ X. ED[ E ]R[ X / I ] ) / I ]
DE[ I = E; D ]R =
  DE[ D ]R[ fix( λ X. ED[ E ](DE[ D ]R[ X / I ]) ) / I ]
```

APPENDIX 2: FLISP SYSTEM FUNCTIONS

FLISP system functions

```
(def assoc (lambda (AssInvoc AssIds)
        (cons   (list (quote lambda) AssIds AssInvoc)
                (mapcar
                    (quote (lambda (AssId)
                            (list (quote quote) (eval AssId))))
                    AssIds
                )
        )
))

(def closure (lambda (CloFun CloIds)
        (list (quote lambda) (car (cdr CloFun))
                (assoc (car (cdr (cdr CloFun))) CloIds)
        )
))

(def suspend (lambda (SuForm SuIds)
        (list (quote su) (assoc SuForm SuIds))
))

(def suspended   (lambda (elem)
        (cond   ((atom elem) nil)
                ((eq (car elem) (quote su)) t)
                (t nil)
        )
))

(def unsu (lambda (elem) (eval (car (cdr elem)))))

(def head (lambda (nvec)
        (cond   ((atom nvec) nil)
                ((suspended (car nvec)) (head (unsu nvec)))
                (t (car nvec))
        )
))

(def tail (lambda (nvec)
        (cond   ((atom nvec) nil)
                ((suspended (car nvec)) (tail (unsu (car nvec))))
                (t (cdr nvec))
        ))
)
```

```
(def concat (lambda (lis1 lis2)
        (cond    ((suspended lis2) (concat lis1 (list lis2)))
                 ((null lis1) lis2)
                 ((suspended lis1) (concat (list lis1) lis2))
                 (t (cons (car lis1) (concat (cdr lis1) lis2)))
        )
))

(def show (lambda (form)
        (prog (lform)
         (setq lform form)
         (cond ((null (atom form)) (go loop)) (t nil))
         (print form)
         (return nil)
         loop
                 (print (head lform))
                 (setq lform (tail lform))
                 (cond ((null lform)  (return nil))
                       (t nil))
                 (print (quote ","))
         (go loop)
         ))
)
```

Note: Ids used here which include upper-case letters should not be
used elsewhere in FLISP programs.

APPENDIX 3: RULES FOR TRANSLATION FROM SUGAR TO FLISP

SUGAR to FLISP translation rules:

S-F0: to translate a program, translate each of the definitions and requested evaluations in order, according to the following rules, replacing any quoted Lambdaexp which might cause violation of the Quote Constraint by an invocation of "closure" with that quoted Lambdaexp as first argument, and with a quoted list of Ids as second argument, those Ids being the ones whose associations are needed for correct evaluation of the Body of that Lambdaexp; any ancillary Defns, such as that for closure, should be included at the start of the translation.

S-F1: name is [args] expr
$$=====> (def\ name\ (lambda\ (\ args'\ )\ expr'\ ))$$
for top-level definitions only

S-F2: name is expr =====> (def name (lambda ( ) expr')
for top-level definitions only, and where expr is not of the form [args] expr; a Lambdaexp with empty Args is known as a parameterless function

S-F3: ([args] expr) (exprs)
=====> ((lambda (args') expr') exprs')
where exprs is a full set of arguments

S-F4: [args] expr =====> (quote (lambda (args') expr'))
except in contexts covered by the previous rules

S-F5: name (exprs) =====> (name exprs')
where exprs is a full set of arguments

S-F6: expr (exprs) =====> (eval (list expr' exprs'))
where expr itself involves function invocation

S-F7: name =====> name
in contexts not covered by earlier rules,
but when name is associated with a parameterless function
name =====> (name), in order to invoke that function

S-F8: $expr_1$, ... , $expr_n$ =====> $expr_1'$ ... $expr_n'$

S-F9: $(expr_1 \text{ op } expr_2)$ =====> $(op' \ expr_1' \ expr_2')$
          but of course a SUGAR operator must be associated with
          its correct operands

S-F10:   **if** $case_1$ **then** $expr_1$ **elsf**...**else** $expr_n$ **endf**
          =====> (cond $(case_1' \ expr_1')$ .... (t $expr_n'$))

S-F11:   {$expr_0$ **where** $name_1$ **is** $expr_1$; ...; $name_k$ **is** $expr_k$}
          =====>
          ((lambda ($name_1$ ... $name_k$) $expr_0'$) $expr_1''$ ... $expr_k''$)
          where the translations $expr_1'', \ldots, expr_k''$ are defined
          as follows:

          for each p, $1 \le p \le k$,
          when $expr_p$ makes no mention of any of $name_1$, ... $name_k$,
              let $expr_p'' = expr_p'$,
                                (obtained by applying rules to $expr_p$),
          when $expr_p$ makes reference to some of $name_1$, ... to $name_k$,
              let $expr_p'' = $ (quote (lambda ( ) $expr_p'$));

          note that within $expr_0'$, $expr_1'$, ... $expr_k'$, occurrences of
          $name_1$, ... $name_k$ must be replaced by $(name_1)$, ... $(name_k)$
          when these are associated with parameterless functions,
          in accordance with S-F7

S-F12: $expr_1$ ($expr_2$) =====> (nth $expr_1' \ expr_2'$)
          when $expr_1$ is a vector, overriding S-F5 and S-F6 in
          this case

S-F13:   < exprs > =====> (list exprs')

S-F14: $expr_1$ && $expr_2$ =====> (concat $expr_1' \ expr_2'$)

S-F15: $expr_1$: $expr_2$ =====> (cons $expr_1' \ expr_2'$)

S-F16:   expr? =====> (show expr')

S-F17:   expr =====> (suspend (quote expr') (quote assocs))
          when expr is an operand of && or : which must be suspended;
          assocs is the list of Ids whose associations are needed
          for correct evaluation of expr'

S-F18:   expr (exprs) =====>
          (closure (quote (lambda (q_1 ... q_m)
                              (expr' exprs' q_1 ... q_m)))
                  (quote (p_1 ... p_n)))
          where less than a full set of arguments is supplied by
          exprs, where m is the number of missing arguments,
          and p_1 ... p_n are the Ids whose associations are needed for
          correct evaluation of exprs'

APPENDIX 4: AN FP SYSTEM IN FLISP

An FP system in FLISP

```
// note: FLISP system defined functions needed to implement closure
//       see APPENDIX 2

// definitions for Combining Forms

(def compose (lambda (f g)
      (closure '(lambda (vcomp) (app f (app g vcomp))) '(f g))
))

(def compo3 (lambda (f g h)
      (closure '(lambda (vcomp)
                       (app f (app g (app h vcomp)))) '(f g h))
))

(def construct (lambda (fseq)
    (closure '(lambda (vconstr)
                    (mapcar '(lambda (fn) (app fn vconstr)) fseq)
              )
            '(fseq))
))

(def toall (lambda (fn)
      (closure '(lambda (vtoall)  (mapcar fn vtoall)) '(fn))
))

(def choose (lambda (testfn trfn falfn)
      (closure
              '(lambda (vchoose)
                  (cond ((testfn vchoose) (trfn vchoice))
                        (t (falfn vchoose))
                  ))
              '(testfn trfn falfn)
      )
))

(def insl (lambda (fn)
      (closure '(lambda (vinsl) (ll fn vinsl)) '(fn))
))

(def insr (lambda (fn)
      (closure '(lambda (vinsr) (lr fn vinsr)) '(fn))
))

(def const (lambda (pconst)
      (closure '(lambda (vconst) pconst) '(pconst))
))
```

223

```
// droptail, lastof are auxiliary functions for lr and ll,
// which are in turn auxiliary for insr, insl,
// which are the Combining Forms rightinsertion, leftinsertion.
// insr will be much more efficient than insl when either
// could be used

(def droptail (lambda (x)
        (cond   ((atom x) nil)
                ((null (cdr x)) nil)
                (t (cons (car x) (droptail (cdr x)))))
        )
))
(def lastof (lambda (x)
        (cond   ((atom x) nil)
                ((null (cdr x)) (car x))
                (t (lastof (cdr x)))
        )
))
(def ll (lambda (fn x)
        (cond   ((atom x) nil)
                ((null (cdr x)) (car x))
                (t (app fn (list (ll fn (droptail x)) (lastof x))))
        )
))
(def lr (lambda (fn x)
        (cond ((atom x) nil)
                ((null (cdr x)) (car x))
                (t (app fn (list (car x) (lr fn (cdr x)))))
        )
))

// now the definitions of Primitive Functions and
//      auxiliary functions.

(def nonpair (lambda (x)
        (cond ((eq x nil) t)
                ((atom x) t)
                ((eq (cdr x) nil) t)
                ((eq (cddr x) nil) nil)
                (t t)
        )
))
(def hd (lambda (x)
        (cond ((atom x) 'undef)
                (t (car x))
        )))
(def tl (lambda (x)
        (cond ((atom x) 'undef)
                (t (cdr x))
        )))
```

```
// sel_n is represented by sel n, so that in fact sel is
// really a Combining Form

(def sel (lambda (n)
        (cond
            ((lessp n 1) 'undef)
            ((eq n 1) 'hd)
            (t (compose (sel (diff n 1)) 't1))
        )))

(def id (lambda (x) x ))

// eqq is used to distinguish from eq in LISP implementation

(def eqq (lambda (x)
        (cond
            ((nonpair x) 'undef)
            (t (equal (car x) (cadr x))))))

(def eq0 (lambda (x) (eqq (list x 0))))

(def gt (lambda (x)
        (cond ((nonpair x) 'undef)
            (t (greaterp (car x) (cadr x))))))

(def ge (lambda (x)
        (cond ((nonpair x) 'undef)
            ((gt x) t)
            ((equal x) t)
            (t nil))))
(def lt (lambda (x)
        (cond ((nonpair x) 'undef)
                (t (lessp (car x) (cadr x)))
        )))

(def le (lambda (x)
        (cond   ((nonpair x) 'undef)
                ((lt x) t)
                ((equal x) t)
                (t nil)
        )))

(def ne (lambda (x)
        (cond   ((nonpair x) 'undef)
                ((equal x) nil)
                (t t)
        )))
```

```
// we assume +, -, *, / can be used as Atoms;
// if not, use pluss, minuss, multt, divv for example

(def + (lambda (x)
       (cond ((nonpair x) 'undef)
             (t (plus (car x) (cadr x))))))

(def - (lambda (x)
       (cond ((nonpair x) 'undef)
             (t (diff (car x) (cadr x))))))

(def * (lambda (x)
       (cond ((nonpair x) 'undef)
             (t (times (car x) (cadr x))))))

(def / (lambda (x)
       (cond ((nonpair x) 'undef)
             (t (quo (car x) (cadr x))))))

(def a (lambda (x)
       (cond ((numbp x) (plus x 1)) (t 'undef))))

(def s (lambda (x)
       (cond ((numbp x) (diff x 1)) (t 'undef))))

(def revaux (lambda (x y)
       (cond ((null y) x)
             (t (revaux (cons (car y) x) (cdr y)))
       )))

(def rev (lambda (x)
       (cond ((null x) x)
             ((atom x) 'undef)
             (t (revaux nil x))
       )))

(def apndl (lambda (x)
       (cond ((nonpair x) 'undef)
             ((eq (cadr x) nil) (list (car x)))
             ((atom (cadr x)) 'undef)
             (t (append (list (car x)) (cadr x)))
       )))

(def apndr (lambda (x)
       (cond ((nonpair x) 'undef)
             ((eq (car x) nil) (list (cadr x)))
             ((atom (car x)) 'undef)
             (t (append (car x) (list (cadr x))))
       )))
```

```
(def distl (lambda (x)
        (cond ((nonpair x) 'undef)
              ((eq (cadr x) nil) nil)
              ((atom (cadr x)) 'undef)
              (t (cons (list (car x) (car (cadr x)))
                       (distl (list (car x) (cdr (cadr x)))))))
        )))
(def distr (lambda (x)
        (cond ((nonpair x) 'undef)
              ((eq (car x) nil) nil)
              ((atom (car x)) 'undef)
              (t (cons (list (caar x) (cadr x))
                       (distr (list (cdar x) (cadr x)))))
        )))

(def transpose (lambda (x)
        (cond   ((atom x) nil)
                ((atom (car x)) nil)
                (t (append (list (app (toall 'hd) x))
                           (transpose (app (toall 'tl) x))))
        )
))

(def andd (lambda (x)
        (cond ((nonpair x) 'undef)
              (t (and (car x) (cadr x)))
        )
))

(def orr (lambda (x)
        (cond ((nonpair x) 'undef)
              (t (or (car x) (cadr x)))
        )))

// selr_n is represented as selr n

(def selr (lambda (n)
        (compose (sel n) 'rev)
))

(def tlr (lambda (x)
        (cond ((atom x) 'undef)
              (t (droptail x))
        )
))
```

```
// range produces list of consecutive integers from x to y

(def range (lambda (x y)
        (cond ((and (numbp x) (numbp y))
                (cond ((eq x y) (list x))
                      ((greaterp x y) nil)
                      (t (cons x (range (plus x 1) y)))))
              (t nil)
        )))

(def iota (lambda (x) (range 1 x)))

// app needed in order to apply a function not given by name.
// e.g. (app (insr '+) (iota 10))

(def app (lambda (f x) (eval (list f 'x))))

// defp used to make FP Definitions
// note that defp also has the effect of associating the body
// of the definition with the name at the outer level, so that
// if the value of such a name is requested, that body will be
// printed out; most systems have a "pretty print" function of
// some kind which might be used to advantage to give more
// readable listing of function definitions

(def defp (lambda (name body)
        (prog
                (eval (list 'def name body))
                (eval (list 'setq name 'body))
        )
))
```

ACCUMULATED BIBLIOGRAPHY

[Bac] Backus J.W. "Can Programming be Liberated from the von Neumann Style? A Functional Style and its Algebra of Programs", Communications of the ACM, Vol. 21, pp. 613-641, August 1978.

[Bar] Barendregt H.P. "The Lambda Calculus — Its Syntax and Semantics", North-Holland, 1981.

[Bu1] Burge W.H. "Recursive Programming Techniques", Addison-Wesley, 1975.

[Bu2] Burstall R.M., McQueen D.B. and Sannella D.T. "HOPE: An experimental applicative language", University of Edinburgh, 1980.

[Chu] Church A. "The Calculi of Lambda-Conversion", Annals of Mathematics Studies No. 6, Princeton University Press, 1941.

[Cla] Clark K.L. and McCabe F.G. "micro-PROLOG: Programming in Logic", Prentice-Hall International, 1984.

[Clo] Clocksin W.F. and Mellish C.S. "Programming in Prolog", Springer-Verlag, 1981.

[Cur] Curry H.B. and Feys R. "Combinatory Logic, Volume 1", North-Holland, 1968.

[Dah] Dahl O.-J., Dijkstra E.W. and Hoare C.A.R. "Structured Programming", Academic Press, 1972.

[Dar] Darlington J., Henderson P. and Turner D.A. "Functional Programming and its Applications", Cambridge University Press, 1982.

[Gor] Gordon M.J.C. "The Denotational Description of Programming Languages", Springer-Verlag, 1979.

[Hen] Henderson P. "Functional Programming: Application and Implementation", Prentice-Hall International, 1980.

[Kin] King M. and Hayes P. "Programming in LISP", in "Computational Semantics" (edited by Charniak E. and Wilks Y.), North-Holland, 1976.

[Kow] Kowalski R. "Logic for Problem Solving", North-Holland, 1979.

[Lan] Landin P.J. "The Next 700 Programming Languages", Communications of the ACM, Vol. 9, pp. 157-166, March 1966.

[Led] Ledgard H. and Marcotty M. "The Programming Language Landscape", Science Research Associates, 1981.

[McC] McCarthy J., Abrahams P.W., Edwards D.J., Hart T.P. and Levin M.I. "LISP 1.5 Programmer's Manual", MIT Press, 1962.

[Man] Manna Z., Ness S. and Vuillemin J. "Inductive Methods for Proving Properties of Programs", Communications of the ACM, Vol. 16, No. 8, August 1973.

[Min] Minsky M.L. "Computation : Finite and Infinite Machines", Prentice-Hall, 1967.

[Pag] Pagan F.G. "Formal Specification of Programming Languages", Prentice-Hall, 1981.

[Sto] Stoy J.E. "Denotational Semantics: The Scott-Strachey Approach to Programming Language Theory", MIT Press, 1977.

[Sus] Sussman G.J. "LISP, Programming and Implementation", in [Dar].

[Te1] Tennent R.D. "Principles of Programming Languages", Prentice-Hall International, 1981.

[Te2] Tennent R.D. "The Denotational Semantics of Programming Languages", Communications of the ACM, Vol. 19, No. 8, August 1976.

[Tre] Treleaven P.C., Brownbridge D.R. and Hopkins R.P. "Data-Driven and Demand-Driven Computer Architecture", ACM Computing Surveys, Vol.14, No.1, March 1982.

[Tur] Turner D.A. "A New Implementation Technique for Applicative Languages", Software Practice and Experience, Vol.9, January 1979.

[Weg] Wegner P. "Programming Languages, Information Structures and Machine Organisation", McGraw-Hill, 1971.

[Wil] Williams J.H. "Notes on the FP style of Functional Programming", in [Dar].

[Wir] Wirth N. "Program Development by Stepwise Refinement", Communications of the ACM, Vol. 14, pp. 221-227, April 1971.

FUNCTION INDEX

INDEX